Stalked

Alison Hewitt originally trained in medical sciences and
nutrition and spent her early twenties travelling the world,
including a stint of voluntary work in India. In 2004 she
decided to follow her passion and study to become
a doctor and today she works as a GP.

Stalked

A life lived in fear. A woman who fought back. A gripping true story.

ALISON HEWITT

PAN BOOKS

*For victims of stalkers, their families
and all those involved in helping
them through their traumas.
May you find peace again.*

First published 2014 by Pan Books

This edition first published 2018 by Pan Books
an imprint of Pan Macmillan
20 New Wharf Road, London N1 9RR
Associated companies throughout the world
www.panmacmillan.com

ISBN 978-1-5290-1606-2

1 3 5 7 9 8 6 4 2

A CIP catalogue record for this book is available from the British Library.

Typeset by Ellipsis Digital Limited, Glasgow
Printed and bound by CPI Group (UK) Ltd, Croydon, CR0 4YY

Visit **www.panmacmillan.com** to read more about all our books
and to buy them. You will also find features, author interviews and
news of any author events, and you can sign up for e-newsletters
so that you're always first to hear about our new releases.

Contents

Prologue

BANG . . . BANG . . . BANG.

The noise exploded in my head like a series of gunshots, ripping through my ears and sending a hot, angry wave of adrenaline bubbling through my veins. My eyes shot open and I jumped out of my skin, scrambling from under the table where I was lying and onto my feet, poised, ready to fight, scream or run.

What the hell was that noise? Had Al broken in? Was he coming for me?

A split second later all was suddenly quiet, and the deafening banging retreated to a soft ticking and gentle whooshing. I realized that the noise was just the sound of the radiator, as the central heating fired up and the water percolated through the pipes right next to where I had been lying on the floor, with my face nestled into the dusty carpet.

I was still alive. I was still safe. It was another day.

It must be early morning. I looked up and could see the

pale yellow sun peeking through the heavy, draped curtains into my ground-floor converted studio flat, sending a stream of iridescent light across the floor.

I reached for my iPhone. I had been clutching it in my right hand as I had fallen asleep, like some sort of comfort blanket. The bright white of the screen glowed back at me – it was just after 6 a.m. I picked it up with my clammy hands and started to type, my fingers working slowly.

The police had 'red-tagged' my phone so I had to check in with them the previous night and first thing in the morning to tell them I was OK and nothing had happened in the night. If I called them, they would be there in a few minutes.

I sent the same message I had just a few hours before, writing: 'I'm fine, no news.'

I did this punctually that morning and evening, since my ex-boyfriend, Al Amin Dhalla, had been arrested while carrying out target practice using a crossbow in a field in Wiltshire. The police found that the weapons Al was using were just within the legal range, so they could only arrest him for driving without a valid licence. All the same, he had been harassing me for months and this new development suggested his behaviour was escalating, and that he was planning something awful.

There was still no news of him. He was still at large. They didn't know where he was but I could sense he was nearby. I don't know how I knew he was, but nowhere felt safe anymore. I watched my back constantly, kept to the main roads when I walked to and from work, and double or triple-checked the different rooms of the flat when I entered. As I made my way to the hospital where I was working as a registrar, I imagined he was following me and would spin round, ready to fight, only to see no one there, except the odd jogger bounding along listening to music or a fellow commuter clutching a handbag or briefcase, pacing their way to their office in the distance. I would quicken my pace until I was practically running, while beads of sweat ran down my back and pooled at the bottom of my spine.

The police were seriously concerned for my safety, which although bringing home to me just how much danger I was in also gave me some comfort. They reassured me that they would do everything they could to help if I needed them and would respond very quickly to my call. They knew as well as I did that Al was a serious threat to me. His behaviour had spiralled seriously out of control.

When I'd lain down on the floor the previous evening, I had kept my clothes and trainers on. The laces were wound and pulled into double knots so tightly that they pinched my feet. I wanted to be ready to sprint if I needed to. I had clutched my phone in my right hand, my index finger hovering above the speed dial button. As I tried to rest, my face staring at the underside of the table and thoughts racing through my mind like a black-and-white film montage on fast forward, I had fully expected to spend a sleepless night tossing and turning, waiting for the morning to arrive. I could feel the adrenaline rushing through my body, heightening every sense, and my heart banged so loudly it echoed in my head. My body tingled uncomfortably, as though an army of insects was prickling my skin from within. The sounds of the wind whistling through the trees outside, the shriek of the seagulls overhead, the neighbours padding around their flat upstairs, the clock ticking mechanically in the kitchen, the beating of my own heart – every small noise was amplified to the point it almost hurt my ears. But somehow in the early hours, I had drifted into a dream-filled sleep, numb and exhausted to my bones.

As I started to wake properly, I blinked hard. With the effects of the adrenaline beginning to wear off, my eyelids felt heavy and cumbersome, like they were too big for my face. I was desperately tired. It was just a few hours earlier that I had arranged my duvet and pillow under a wooden table in my living room – the place I considered safest. My flat was compact and there was only one escape route – through the front door. The bedroom had large, high Victorian windows and I knew if Al tried to fire a weapon through them, he would hit the bullseye immediately. I decided that if he came hammering through the front door, he would dash past me without looking to his side, thinking I would be curled up asleep in the bed we once shared.

My flat was once my safe haven and when I used to step through the front door it was like it hugged me. Now, it felt cold and lonely and like I had never lived there at all.

I tried not to be too frightened, but whenever I succeeded the same thoughts would pop back into my head and I would become a bag of nerves once more. If Al had bought a crossbow once, he could get one again. It would be easy enough. Whatever he had intended to do to me, he would try again, I was sure of it.

I had briefly considered staying with one of my friends, bundling up a few belongings into a bag and making a phone call, but I couldn't put anyone I knew at risk. I knew I was vulnerable, although looking back I question whether it had really sunk in just how much I was gambling with my safety by staying there. I had shut down and rather than feel terrified, I felt absent, as though all that was left of me was an empty shell. I couldn't cope with the inevitable hysteria from my friends about what was happening. I didn't want to talk about it over endless cups of lukewarm coffee and answer the same questions: did I not see the warning signs? Why hadn't I finished the relationship sooner? What might happen next? Could I not tell he was a maniac? So instead I kept my feelings and fears bottled up inside, choosing not to tell anyone outside my family the full details of the situation.

I didn't want to talk about it, think about it or live it. I just wanted to get on with my life and work was the one thing that was keeping me going. Work meant I had to get up in the morning, have a shower, put on some clothes and somehow put one foot in front of the other, step outside the front door and make my way to the hospital. However tempted I was to hide under the table, curl up and never come out, I knew I had to keep some semblance of my former life. And anyway, I knew there was no point: Al would find me wherever I was. He would track me down if I moved in with a friend, if I went on holiday for a few weeks, retreated back to my child-hood home or even if I went into hiding for weeks or months. He was so fixated with me, obsessed to the point of insanity.

He was like a completely different person from the one I

had first met. The man I had once loved had turned into a monster I barely recognized. I found it hard to reconcile these two men in my mind: Mr Dhalla, who was making my life a living hell, and Al, the fun and easy-going guy who had wooed me with exciting trips and dinners at smart restaurants. At one time, before I discovered who he truly was, I had loved him.

While none of us knew exactly what he had been plotting in the background, I think my family thought exactly the same as I did: that whatever the plan was, it was something way beyond anything we had seen from him before. He was clearly working towards some sort of end game. Beneath his seemingly calm, verbose and confident exterior, he wanted me for himself – and he would use whatever means necessary to get me.

One

The Agency

'A dating agency is the answer, Alison, seriously.'

I was sitting with my friend Kate in a coffee shop in London's Soho and we were discussing how to tackle my love life. It was November 2009 and as I looked outside the window, which seemed to sag with the moisture of bodies and talking, every smeared outline seemed to be of a couple huddled underneath an umbrella or a man ushering his other half along the pavement, out of the way of the black taxis and bicycles weaving up the dirt-strewn, narrow roads. Next to us an older couple sat deep in whispered conversation, their hands and fingers entwined tightly across the coffee-splashed table, their drinks abandoned long before.

I had decided the time had arrived. I was thirty-five and had been single for a few months, and I had not had a really serious boyfriend for a number of years. I knew that I wanted to meet someone special, have a meaningful relationship and think about settling down, getting married and having a family. I wanted to meet the man who I could imagine myself walking down the aisle towards and saying 'until death do us part' to. Deep down, don't most women long for that day? I wanted my umbrella moment.

'You know I met Jack through that exclusive London agency I told you about,' Kate continued. 'And that relationship lasted for eighteen months. He was great: funny, handsome and he treated me amazingly. He'll always be the one that got away.'

I just wasn't the sort of girl who was going to meet someone in an overcrowded bar or sweaty nightclub. I hated the sticky floors, forced conversations and bad hangovers the next morning. With finishing my training and qualifying as a fully fledged doctor being the number one priority in my life at that point, late nights were becoming increasingly rare and I no longer really enjoyed going out like I used to back in my twenties. My social life in Brighton, where I lived, had morphed into a more sedate round of drinks after work with medical colleagues or meeting at friends' houses for dinner, where everyone brought a dish along to share.

I had not long finished my first stint of four months in a GP's office and had loved it. I had run my own clinics, seen emergency patients and gone on home visits with another doctor to those patients who couldn't get into the surgery for one reason or another. We also went to a nearby old people's home to diagnose any problems and dish out prescriptions. I was still in my first year of GP training but I loved the variety involved in seeing every age group, from newborns with their tiny, perfect fingers and toes, right the way through to centenarians, with wizened faces, witty comments and enchanting stories.

Socially, I've always been a people person, casting my net wide when it comes to making and maintaining friendships, and I found doctoring satisfied my sociable side. And while I was ambitious, like most doctors who have sat through years of burying their heads in their textbooks and studying for exams, I had been happy to be away from the hierarchical nature of hospitals. I have always found that they are places where a few enormous egos are allowed to cause waves, and some individuals are so desperate to make their next move up the greasy ladder they have no qualms about pushing anyone in their path firmly out of their way, letting their own voice be heard above all others.

I considered Kate's comment, and felt that maybe the route she was suggesting would be a good idea for my lifestyle.

'All the men are vetted by the agency, so there won't be any weirdos?' I asked.

'No, they check everyone out and ask all sorts of stuff – not just the basics like your job and what you are looking for, but they even ask about your finances and health. They are very thorough. You will meet the right type of man, the sort you could easily take home and show off to your family – or even marry', she continued. 'There's absolutely no chance of them hooking you up with a womanizing busker with just a manky dog and a few pounds to his name, let's put it that way.'

For a while I had considered Internet dating. I know loads of people meet people and date online, including some of my friends, but deep down I'm quite a shy person and, in an old-fashioned way, I was concerned about my privacy. The thought of hundreds of men looking at my pictures and reading about my life would make me feel somehow exposed. I had also heard some real horror stories: a friend of a friend went on four dates with one seemingly lovely guy before he admitted he had been married for ten years and had three young children, and a colleague's phone was flooded with dodgy, pornographic pictures and pleading text messages after one innocent coffee meet-up.

The other major factor in play was lack of time; Kate knew that my job meant that I didn't have loads of time to trawl through profiles and, not having a desk job, I wasn't able to sneak a look at my personal stuff when work was quiet. Work was never quiet. Having finished my stint at the GP's office, I had just started working back at the main hospital in the renal ward and it was pretty manic. I did shift work, which included many 6 a.m. starts, staying right through to 6 p.m., with only a couple of short breaks if I was lucky. Often I was on call from when my shift finished until midnight, so it didn't exactly leave much room for dating.

I was mainly working on the ward with patients who had kidney failure. Many of them were very sick and dependent upon dialysis. Some would recover but many faced life-changing treatment and needed dialysis three times a week or were desperately awaiting a donor kidney match as their only hope of survival. The work was complex and highly specialized. I would follow the jobs list set out by the consultant, who was in charge to make sure everything was done accurately, timely and well. I was normally given a bay of patients

– about eight people – to look after and if, unusually, I finished early for any reason, I would help out my colleagues, and they would do the same if they somehow made it through their list of tasks before I did. It was also challenging work because there were always worried families hovering around and asking lots of questions, which I would try to answer as best I could. I had been taught, like other doctors, never to sugar-coat the truth, but to offer up the facts as clearly and as kindly as I could. So it was busy and demanding, and the idea of finding a computer in any spare time I had and logging on to a dating site to check out my 'winks' or 'pokes', or if Bob from London had given my profile the thumbs up, seemed faintly ridiculous.

'It sounds like it really cuts out the legwork?' I asked tentatively.

'It really does. And it's good fun. Before Jack, I met a couple of other guys and I didn't fancy them, but they were both nice. It's a great way of meeting lots of different types of people.'

'So what's the catch?'

'There's no catch,' she explained. 'They make it really easy for you. If you don't like the date they set you up with, you let them know and they find you another match. You just move on until you find someone you have a connection with. You should date anyone once.'

The conversation moved on as we caught up on six months' worth of news. Kate was a friend I had met when travelling through Thailand in my twenties and we had got to know one another on a trip from Bangkok to Singapore, bonding over our nasty mosquito bites and sickness. After a particularly vigorous hike to one temple at the top of a huge mountain, I'd succumbed to dehydration and Kate had quickly ferried me to the doctors and played nurse back at the hostel where we were lodging. She was someone I became very close to and I stayed with her family when I spent some time in New Zealand. After our respective travels, Kate had eventually relocated to London and set herself up for a few years with a good job and a rented room in Queen's Park, but now was heading back to her native New Zealand to settle down and hopefully meet her life partner. She filled me in on what she was planning to do once she got home and all about leaving her work and temporary digs in London behind.

I told her more about my life in Brighton and the work I was doing in the hospital. By that point, I had been living in my flat on the south coast for a year and loved everything about the place, from the breathtaking scenery of the undu-lating South Downs and the salty air you inhaled while walking along the beach, to the kooky shops, crazy fashions and the anything-goes, bohemian feel. In one of the flats opposite mine there was a transvestite with bad stubble rash and a rugby prop's torso who wore the same pencil skirt and bad blue eyeshadow every day, but no one batted an eyelid. For me, it was the perfect blend of town and country living.

When I'd decided to study for my medicine degree, I had hoped to go to Brighton University to be by the sea but they couldn't offer me funding. When the University of Warwick made me a funded offer I just couldn't turn it down, but during the years I was there I hatched a plan that I would eventually move to Brighton to complete my training after I had finished the first part of my degree. When I first moved, I'd found my rented flat, which was just a couple of roads from the seafront, in a small block at the end of the driveway of a far grander house.

I also gave Kate the lowdown on my most recent relationship. While some of my friends were mad about pubs, shopping and going out, for me, I was happiest outdoors, exploring different parts of the countryside. I loved the fresh air, the way it cleared my mind and made me feel calm and centred. Shortly after I landed in Brighton, I joined an adventure sports group covering London and the South East, in part to have fun and stay fit but also in the hope I'd meet someone who had similar interests to my own. I threw myself head first into a lot of the activities the club put on locally, like hiking days, climbing trips and sailing courses, and through one of those days out, I'd met a guy called Tom, who I had dated for a couple of months. He was a police detective working in London and shared my passion for outdoor pursuits. His main love was sailing and he owned a boat and took it out as much as he could. One weekend, he took me across the Solent to the Isle of Wight and he was keen to get me up to speed on all things boat-related, explaining what all the equipment on the boat did and about the science of rudders, headwinds and tacking. On other weekends when there was at least a hint of sunshine, he took me out on shorter trips and charged me with pulling different ropes, letting various sails in and out and ensuring I ducked at the right time, so I didn't get a bruised forehead!

Of course, we spent a lot of time talking about our jobs and careers. His work with the police focused around gang crime, domestic violence and illegal drugs. It was clear that sailing was his way of escaping his job and the barbarity of the things he saw every day. He spoke at length about innocent teenagers who had been knifed, savage gang crime initiations and early morning drug raids. His chatter made me feel uncomfortable and awkward.

After a few dates, I decided I found the brutality of his everyday life just too much; I didn't enjoy hearing his stories and started to resent the explicit detail he offered up, almost like everyday gossip. He was also quite flashy and owned a beautiful, huge house in West London and had a shiny convertible car parked in the driveway, which was his pride and joy. This kind of showy lifestyle wasn't very 'me'; I've never been bothered about what kind of car I own or if I'm carrying the latest designer handbag. Both these differences between us left me feeling that it wasn't right, so in the end I'd let it fizzle out. It was all very amicable and we still saw each other with the group. Not long afterwards, he'd started dating another doctor, a psychiatrist, and they both seemed very happy to have found each other, so I was pleased for him.

The group had lots of events going on further afield but I was often limited as to how far I could travel because of work, and after spending all day in the hospital racing up and down the ward with a head full of my complex 'to do' list, I didn't feel particularly excited about embarking on a two-hour car journey every weekend, so I knew that my quest to meet someone had to take another route. I hoped to meet someone who was more local on the south coast, and I imagined – and hoped – that there were probably a lot of eligible men living near me, who, like me, lacked the time to date.

As Kate and I left and hugged each other firmly, promising to keep in touch when she arrived back in New Zealand, she laughed, 'I'm going to text you the name of the agency now, so you've got it on your phone. Even if you don't find your perfect man, you will've had a nice time. Remember what I said: you should date anybody once. When I speak to you when I'm home, I want to know that you are on their books, no excuses.'

'OK. I'll look later,' I promised.

She raised one quizzical and perfectly groomed eyebrow and laughed. 'Really?'

'I will,' I said. 'Who knows? The next time we see each other I might be instructing you to buy a new hat.'

In my flat later that night, after mindlessly flicking through the channels on the TV and tuning into reruns of *Come Dine with Me* and *Murder, She Wrote*, I checked my phone and scrolled down to Kate's message. It read: 'The Executive Club of St James's. Do it!'

I moved over to the dining table and fired up my laptop, which flickered to life with a sonorous ring. I typed the agency name into Google; the title sounded impressive enough and the banner read 'London's outstanding dating agency for professionals'. An old-fashioned-looking website crammed with pictures of couples holding hands over white tablecloths and walking into the sunset with the sand beneath their toes lit up my screen. It piqued my interest and I started reading. It said it was an agency for younger professionals, which is unusual apparently because mostly dating agencies cater for older singles in their forties onwards. There seemed to be an emphasis on the fact that the members of The Executive Club of St James's were looking for long-term commitment, not just guys wanting flings or women seeking a man to take them on expensive mini-breaks.

As I scrolled down, I came to the section entitled 'So Why Should Women Join Us?' It read: 'We hold the most intensive interview in the industry, during which we screen out the sort of guys that waste your time.' The agency would weed out the married men posing as single and the men who were just players, and introduce women to 'the five guys of the quality you would be proud to meet'.

Men who subsequently proved unreliable were removed from the list. According to the agency, 'ALL of our men are intelligent, emotionally strong, successful, genuinely unattached and seriously looking for a long-term partner.'

It sounded a bit serious and OTT but I was hopeful that joining an agency like this would push me to go on more dates so I could meet someone who I clicked with. Their criteria stated that you had to be aged between twenty-three and forty-three, a professional person, and men had to be at least 5 foot 6. I ticked all the boxes. After browsing for a few minutes, my phone started buzzing, and I swiftly shut my laptop with one hand and quickly forgot about it.

*

A week or so later, after some rudely early starts for work where I had dragged myself from the warm cocoon of my bed and trekked in the dark to the hospital for my shifts, I found myself once again lying flat on my sofa with no plans for the evening. I thought of all of my friends snuggling up with their boyfriends on their sofas, hand in hand, chatting about their days, and I felt a sharp pang of loneliness. But there was no use moping, I decided. I had a few hours to kill and the thought of the agency came into my mind.

Did I really want to go on loads of dates? Unlike some of my female friends who got chatted up everywhere, even when browsing the carrots in the vegetable aisle at Tesco's during their weekly shop or filling up their cars at the petrol pump, I have never been someone who is asked out all the time. I also have never gone out with lots of different guys and played the field. I knew I needed a change of attitude. I had always met new people in my twenties because I had gone travelling, and in the latter years went back to university to do my medicine degree. However, with my roots now firmly entrenched in Brighton those meetings, where you caught the eye of a friend of a friend across a bar or a fellow student across the lecture theatre and felt that spark of attraction, had wound down to a halt. There were no new romantic prospects on the horizon and I felt I had nothing to lose. I needed to put myself out there. Going down the route of an agency seemed to make complete sense because it would make my life easier.

I am going to do this, I told myself. *No more procrastinating.*

I booted up my laptop and went straight to the agency's website, navigating to the 'Contact Us' and 'FAQ' pages. There was a range of membership options and none of them were cheap – in fact, some of the more so-called 'exclusive' services extended into thousands of pounds – but I was quite happy to pay out of my hard-earned salary because I felt that the fee would automatically put off any timewasters and it seemed that it was justified through the amount of time the agency spent trying to find suitable matches and vetting people. I decided it was an investment in my future.

After calling and having a chat with a well-spoken and upbeat lady, who took down my details and said someone would call me back to talk further, I felt positive and excited about what lay ahead. *This is it*, I said to myself. *This is the beginning of a whole new chapter.*

A week or so later, I met the owner of the agency, a man called Alun, for a drink and to talk more about the agency and how the process worked. By chance Alun lived and worked along the south coast, so we agreed to meet at his office which was a short walk from my flat, near the seafront. He was an older gentleman but was smart and professional, with a kind and open face. He asked me general information about myself, such as my age and job, but also probed further into my life, enquiring after my finances and health. Although he was very polite, the level and the intensity of his questioning, such as his enquiries about my sexual health, left me a bit perplexed but I reassured myself that it was a good thing because everyone on the agency's books would be asked the same sorts of things. There would be no timewasters going through that process. He finished off by telling me more about the agency and asking me about my relationship history.

'So, what type of person are you looking for exactly, Alison?' he asked.

I took a large sip of tea. 'I'm not 100 per cent sure,' I answered. 'Someone kind and caring, intelligent and thoughtful; someone who likes to discuss the deeper issues in life but who I can also have fun with. All I know is that I haven't met anyone who quite fits the bill yet.'

I took another sip of tea and began to give him a potted overview of my romantic history. My first serious relationship was with a guy called James who I had met during my first year at Leeds University, where I was studying for my medical science degree. He was living in my halls for his final year so he could be on campus and get his head down. Like most eager newbies, I had stumbled around during freshers' week signing up for some random clubs with the promise of good-looking men and free alcohol, and in my first term I found myself doing kung fu classes with one of James's friends. Eventually the friend introduced me to James one night at the union bar. There was an instant attraction and after a few drinks, then a dinner date, we started going out.

Physically, he was as skinny as a rake and extremely tall; I delighted in buying pairs of ridiculously high heels for a while. Like me, he had fair hair, and he was quite clean cut. I liked the fact he was a bit different; not your typical beer-swigging, football-watching student, delighting in being away from home for the first time. He was very fit and was really into his martial arts, with many various coloured belts taking pride of place in his cupboard. On nights out I felt very protected as he put his arm around me, imagining he would high-kick or karate chop anyone who came near me. He was also a keen runner, sometimes waking up at the crack of dawn to sprint around the university athletics track with a tyre on his back in some sort of mad quest for ultimate fitness. He was a brilliant guitar player too and fancied himself as a bit of a Noel Gallagher, so we spent many evenings in his room with our other friends, the air thick with smoke, while he strummed away and we sang along badly. The relationship lasted for most of the year but when James started burying himself in his books as his finals approached, and I wanted more of his attention and began to feel neglected, it gradually ended. After the long summer holidays, when I went to Africa and he settled himself into London life with a room in a flatshare and a new job, he called wanting to rekindle things, but I wasn't interested. I wanted more freedom and knew that dating him would mean travelling down to London every weekend to see him. But mostly I think we'd just grown too far apart by that point.

The next serious romance happened about a year later, just after I'd finished uni. After Leeds I moved up to Aberdeen for a year to study for a master's degree in nutrition and I met Ajay, who was from Barbados, at a party. The attraction was blinding and unlike anything I had experienced before. I finally understood the term 'blown away' and what all those famous songs about lust, love and romance really meant.

I would hang on his every word, count down the hours until I saw him and think about him constantly during lectures. At the time, we were both still really young and despite our mutual attraction we decided that we didn't want anything too serious and classed our relationship as more of a 'fling'.

As it happened I think I was more into Ajay than I let on to anyone – including myself. As well as having incredible dark olive-coloured eyes that I found hypnotizing at times, he was just so much fun to be around. He shared a house with five other guys and I shared my house – which was just a couple of roads away – with five girls. We spent many nights partying at each other's houses, dressing up in fancy dress, playing drinking games and whiling away the hours; in fact, looking back, it seemed like one long celebration.

Ajay was away from home for the first time and delighted in every new thing: from the frost – he loved the feeling of being cold, having only ever experienced the burning sunshine year-round – to Scottish food, like haggis and black pudding. I remember vividly someone saying one time that there was the possibility of seeing the Northern Lights a few miles north of where we lived and, egged on by Ajay, we bundled into someone's car late that night and sat on the beach for hours. It felt like it must've been about minus-10 and while we were wearing the warmest clothes we could find and were all huddled together in an attempt to stop our teeth chattering, I remember that Ajay couldn't stop smiling as he was so excited at the prospect of seeing the Lights, even just a glimmer of them. As it was, we didn't get to witness the spectacular light show, but Ajay still didn't stop smiling. He never did, whatever the situation. His teeth always glowed as he grinned from ear to ear. I found his viewpoint on life really interesting and refreshing.

In the end, after he finished studying, Ajay moved down to London and we called time on our relationship because of the distance and the fact that he eventually wanted to head back to the blue waters of the Caribbean, but for the six months we were together, I was probably the happiest I have been with anyone.

'Looking back, I was pretty smitten,' I told Alun, smiling.

After university I decided to go travelling. I have always had a burning passion to discover different countries and cultures. I never wanted to be a tourist with a phrase book in one hand and a crumpled map in the other, trekking along with the other tourists like a flock of sheep being herded in the heat to the obvious destinations. I always hoped to fully submerge myself in the cultures, like a diver rolling blindly backwards off an inflatable boat into the sea. I wanted to find out what was at the heart of people's lives; their particular customs, their history and what made them tick; why they made certain choices regarding careers, lifestyles or families. I wanted to have my eyes opened to the world beyond the small one I knew.

I started my travels in Budapest, then went on to Japan, and in both places I taught English to fund my tours. I finished my adventures in India, where I worked with a charity for street children. While I had jobs in Budapest and Japan that paid, I didn't want to be an ex-pat who hung out in the ex-pat bars flashing an inflated salary, so I lived very modestly in spare rooms of local families, worked during the day for a reasonable pay cheque at the end of the month and went out to nearby restaurants and bars at night.

When I was in Hungary, I met a French guy called Louis, who I was very close to for a year, but it was more platonic than anything. He was keen to take the romance further but for some reason, even though I was hugely fond of him, we never really got off the starting blocks. I just didn't feel the same, and after a trip to France together, where I discovered that I found everything from his accent to the way he tied his laces grating, that was that. In Japan I had another fairly long-term romance with an American guy but I didn't want anything to hold me back from enjoying life to the fullest. At that time I think I saw relationships as binding and thought they would stop me doing what I wanted, so I never took them very seriously. It wasn't that I didn't want to be tied down to one person or I found it difficult to be faithful; I just didn't want to be shackled to one place for too long. All I was interested in was adventure and discovering new places.

'But I feel differently now,' I told Alun. 'I really feel ready to make that change. I love my life in Brighton but the one thing that would make it better would be someone to enjoy my free time with.'

He nodded as I continued to tell him more about myself. In 2004, when I was twenty-nine, I finally decided to pursue another long-held ambition and train to become a doctor. Doing another degree was a massive decision and would mean many more years of studying, and a huge financial commitment as I would end up running up some debts to cover my fees and living expenses. I knew if I took the plunge then I would have to get my head down and work harder than I ever had before. Travelling, going out and having fun were going to have to be put on the backburner as I buried myself in textbooks.

'So I'm seven years in to my studies now,' I added, 'and the time feels right. I'm really settled in Brighton now, so it would be good to meet someone who didn't live too far away.'

'OK, great,' he said. 'And can I ask you more about what you are looking for in a potential partner?'

What was I looking for? I guess like most women, old and young, I was after that big, fat cliché: I hoped to meet some-one who I was physically attracted to; who was kind, caring, funny and solvent, with a bright future. They would need to know who they were, where they were going and what they wanted out of life.

'That's a good attitude,' Alun explained. 'We try to get our female members away from thinking they want to meet a six-foot Brad Pitt-lookalike who is a banker and concert pianist in his free time, and to focus more on what type of man they want in their lives.

'A big part of this process for you will be going on lots of dates with different men and thinking more about your wish list. And of course, everyone is vetted in the same way. We have some very eligible men on our books, so you won't be disappointed. There is a reason I talk about being proud of our members. That is genuinely how I feel about them.'

Getting out there and meeting a range of new people was what I had told myself I would do. I remembered Kate's words about dating anybody once and I agreed.

During our talk, Alun told me more about the agency and how the process would work. He explained that I wouldn't see pictures of my potential dates and they wouldn't see any of me. We would just be given some information about the other person and if we both liked the sound of each other, then someone from the agency would ask permission to pass our phone numbers on so we could talk further about meeting up.

'So I or someone in my office will be in touch in the next couple of days when we find a suitable match for you, Alison. Good luck.'

As I walked back along the beach, sharing it with lone runners and dog walkers, I felt really buoyant.

This was a new start for me. I hadn't felt this excited in a long time.

Two

First Impressions

I could feel the November chill through the draught from my bedroom window when I woke, so I lay in bed a while longer wondering what the day held in store. It had been two weeks since my meeting with Alun and my first date through the agency was arranged for that evening.

I knew there was no point in bluffing or pretending to be someone I wasn't; I needed to throw myself wholeheartedly into the process and be straightforward about exactly what I wanted. Hopefully I would find that elusive person who would make me feel like Ajay did all that time ago, yet that person would be set up in their life, like me, with a clear idea of what they wanted their future to look like. If I met that man, I would happily jump in feet first and throw out the timeline, say goodbye to the rule book and the ticking clock, and just be myself and move at the speed I wanted to.

After a brief phone call, I'd arranged to meet Frank, who lived in Lewes, Brighton's somewhat quieter and smaller neighbour, for a drink at a local place near my flat. As soon as I clapped eyes on the skinny guy sitting in the corner nursing his coffee, I just knew there would be no spark. I went over and said 'Hi' and while the conversation wasn't strained and he was a perfectly good guy, it was clear I was never going to cut it as his Mrs Right and vice versa. For a start, while I had promised myself to think less about physical attraction, he was far too short and skinny for me. I mentally calculated that his thighs were about the width of my arm and that I probably weighed at least two stone more than him. This was not good. However, I told myself, I needed to do this, so we drank our mochas and made small talk. Our interests were wildly different; he started waxing lyrical about his passion for art, critiquing various exhibitions he had seen, including one by a local watercolour painter and another by a Turner Prize winner. I didn't feel I had much to add and scrambled around in my brain for something insightful and astute to say. From time to time I would look round a gallery if I liked the sound of an exhibition, and I either liked the pictures or I didn't. This was much the same way I felt about his other passion, which was wine. He considered himself quite an expert, he admitted, and had started investing in fine wines with Berry Bros. & Rudd. When I mentioned my love of the outdoors, he just looked blankly back at me. We wrapped it up fairly quickly and said our goodbyes. It was clear this wasn't a match.

While Frank wasn't my cup of tea, far from feeling deflated, I left the date feeling optimistic. So what if we didn't fancy each other? It was only the first date I'd been on, after all. It wasn't so bad and I had actually quite enjoyed his company.

Over the weeks that followed, I had a couple of phone calls about possible 'matches'. Someone from the agency would ring to tell me a bit about the other person, including their name, job and little bit of extra information about them, which was whatever they had given the agency permission to say. For me, they would say that my name was Alison and I was a doctor, living and working in Brighton, and my passions included outdoor pursuits and travelling. I had specified that I hoped to meet someone between the age of thirty-three and forty but neither age nor looks were ever discussed during those phone calls.

One evening, a week or so before Christmas, my phone buzzed. It was one of the ladies from the agency, suggesting another match for me.

'One of our members is called Al,' she said. 'He's Canadian and has been in London for five years. He works as an insurance broker in London and he loves the outdoors and is interested in history. Would you like to meet him?'

'Yes, sure,' I answered.

'Great, so I have your permission to pass on your number?'

'Yes,' I replied, thinking that he sounded promising. Again I thought, *What have I got to lose?*

After my shift in the renal ward on Christmas Eve, I headed back to my family home to celebrate with my mum and her partner, David. I grew up living in a pretty thatched cottage in the picturesque village of Aston Abbotts, near Aylesbury in

Buckinghamshire. It's a beautiful and homely house. Part of the building is over 500 years old and it is directly opposite the village church. When we moved there in the 1980s when I was eleven, from a small village called Styrrup in South Yorkshire, my dad and another villager spent a long time renovating and extending the house to make it habitable for us. I think the only way that my parents could afford to up sticks with four young children and move south was to do a house up. For six long weeks we all lived in an enormous static caravan in a field nearby, while the building work took place. I think it was pretty grim for Mum but we loved the sense of adventure. I have vague memories of starting a new school and the other children asking me if we were gypsies and where we went to the loo.

Now I was in Brighton and doing a rotation of placements as part of my training, I only made it back to my mum's house every few months for Sunday lunch. It was – and very much still is – my home; the one place, other than the flat, that I can raid the cupboard for biscuits or help myself to endless cups of coffee and relax in front of the Aga or enormous wood burner in the sitting room.

The village of Aston Abbotts is also a bit of an extension of the family, at least for Mum and David. There is a very active local community and the people are approachable and friendly. The population is less than 500 and there is a very busy church and a pub called The Royal Oak. David goes to The 630 Club at the pub most Saturdays with the men in the village and Mum attends the ladies' equivalent, GNOMES (Girls Night Out Men Excluded Sorry), too. They have a traditional village fete complete with tombola, coconut shy and bunting in the summer, an annual harvest festival, a fireworks display on Bonfire Night and annual summer and New Year's Eve balls, where everyone puts on their glad rags and dances the night away. The village seems to exist in its own happy, glossy bubble, where the people are very good friends and always look out for one another.

I was born in December 1974 and I'm the eldest child of the family. Mark came along a little more than eighteen months later, in August 1976, and Paul followed in February 1980. Finally David, who I call Dave, made an appearance in June 1982. The four of us grew up in a very happy home. We all passed the entrance exams for the local grammar schools, so I went off to Aylesbury High at twelve, and the boys were at Aylesbury Grammar. I was very studious, worked hard and always had my head in a book. During my GCSE years I would insist Mum took me to the library after school, so I could study in peace away from my brothers. She says that she never had to worry about me during my teenage years and, far from going off the rails, she was concerned that I didn't have enough fun! My free time was mostly taken up with music; I had piano and violin lessons during the week and practised religiously. I eventually made it to Grade 8 on the piano and even though I was never a particularly gifted violinist I spent lots of weekends sitting at the back of the local youth orchestra with the other second violins, trying to keep up with the rest of the impressive string section.

Both Mum and Dad worked; Dad was a social worker and

later taught social workers at university and, when we were younger, Mum worked part-time as a probation officer and social worker. In the latter part of her career, she worked as a senior lecturer in higher education teaching psychology. Like me, the boys were always busy doing something or other – they were into computers and sport – so most of Mum and Dad's free time in the evenings and at weekends was spent ferrying us all to our various clubs and extracurricular activities.

During the long summer holidays, we would all pile into the car with all our belongings and drive down to Brittany, where we would camp in this huge family tent and go off to all the various clubs during the day to give my parents some peace. In the evenings we would cook seafood on the barbecue and teach the French children how to play cricket. We all loved getting out and about, making new friends and practising our French. I guess these holidays are what sparked my love of travelling.

When we were growing up Mum and Dad were very loving and supportive of us all in our individual ways. Dad was the disciplinarian and stricter than Mum, although he often spoilt us and I have one vivid memory of him buying me some clothes as a teenager, which I'm sure my mum would have thought were unnecessary. Tragically we lost my dad very suddenly due to a heart complication in January 1996, when I was just twenty-one and still at university – both Paul and Dave were still at school. It was an awful, devastating time for all of us. When it happened I didn't know how we'd ever get through it, but I knew I had to be practical, like Dad always was, and just carry on, and somehow we managed to pull ourselves back together.

A few years later Mum met David, my now stepfather, and we are all very close, despite the fact two of my brothers now live overseas: Mark in Norway with his family and Dave in Sydney, Australia. Mark is quite self-contained and quiet, like me. With a degree in computer science, he's a self-confessed computer geek and is extremely hard working. He's the sort of person who seems to have sailed quite happily through the plotted journey of life. He did well at school, went on to university and has always had good jobs. He had his heart broken by his first proper girlfriend at university not long after Dad died, and Mum says she was terrified that he would never recover, especially when he didn't call home for three weeks. But, as it turns out, less than seven days after the break-up he met his now wife, Paula. After getting married they moved to Stavanger in Norway and have three gorgeous boys called Matthew, Fraser and James.

Dave, the baby of the family, is far more outgoing and fun-loving than the rest of us; he's the life and soul of the party. He's had a variety of jobs including working in estate agents, building societies and banks, but he's finally ended up with the job of his dreams, working in the marketing department at Google in Sydney, which suits his fun and sparky personality to a T. He's very happy-go-lucky and once described his job to me as 'taking people out and getting pissed'.

Dave and I are really close – despite the fact he's geographically a long way away. Since he was little we have always got on. As a kid, I found Paul and Mark quite annoying because they were always careening around being boisterous and playing on their computer games with their friends. They delighted in winding me up and most of the time, at least when we were out, I liked to walk a couple of feet ahead of them so no one associated them with me! When we were all in the house together, Dave and I would hole up somewhere and shut the wooden door as firmly as we could in an attempt to get away from the noise. I've always felt very protective of Dave, and when our dad died I felt even more strongly that I should be there for him. Unlike most men, he's great at keeping in touch. Given the nature of his work, he's always on Facebook tracking all his friends and updating his timeline with pictures and comments, so I know what he's doing, and we text and Skype as much as possible. He returns home about once a year, so we always get together during one of his whirlwind tours, where he catches up with his friends and all of us.

Last but by no means least, there's Paul, the non-conformist member of the family. He's a real free spirit who embraces the outdoors lifestyle, but in an altogether different way to me. He lives in a caravan or on his boat, which he bought second-hand. For a time shortly after the purchase we were all beside ourselves with worry that it might sink in the canal where it is based because the bottom of the boat was so rusty. He's full of ideas and dreams and always has a new scheme in the pipeline, some of which never really come to fruition. He's got a heart of gold and would give the shirt off his back to someone who needed it – literally. Once, when we went to the Gambia on holiday, Mum bought him some new clothes for the occasion and at the airport, before we returned home, he revealed he had left all his clothes behind because the people there 'needed them more'. Mum had to bite her lip. On another occasion, in Cambodia, he ferried all of the unwanted food from the hotel kitchen out to the masses of starving people in the outskirts of the village where he was staying, like a one-man humanitarian aid mission.

Mum is always happier when Paul has a girlfriend because he is 'much better behaved', and at least then she can get hold of him – years have gone past when he hasn't owned a mobile phone and no one has known where to locate him. The girl-friends in his life seem to come and go but the one permanent fixture is his beloved dog, Linus, a handsome Rhodesian ridgeback. He's large and slim like a greyhound, with a beau-tiful regal face and a sharp glint in his sooty eyes, like he knows a lot about everything. A few years ago Paul started dating a young single mother, but after a while things weren't going well. The final nail in the coffin was when her child yanked Linus's tail when he was asleep and he snapped back. This was not the first time the child had tormented the dog, and the mother hadn't told her son off. She then declared, 'It's me or the dog.' That was a big mistake, of course, because without even thinking about it Paul chose Linus, and swiftly called time on that relationship. She should've known better than to issue that ultimatum. I hope he'll meet someone who makes him happy and loves Linus as much as he does, and we fully expect him to one day announce out of the blue that he has got married through the process of crossing some sticks in the middle of a field during a full moon!

While Paul doesn't own a television or a credit card and only uses a phone sporadically, it's almost guaranteed that he will turn up at the front door at important times like Christmas, when there is the smell of delicious food wafting out of the kitchen and the house remains mostly unchanged from when we were children growing up there.

Christmases at home were always very traditional when we were growing up, especially when Dad was still alive. We always woke early and excitedly opened our stockings. Each year we would get a couple of fun toys that we wanted alongside a selection of practical items, like toothbrushes, toothpaste, socks, pants and deodorant. We would always cross the road to the village church for the service and to sing carols. The standout moment when we were kids was when we were given colourful, foil-wrapped chocolates from the tree and then afterwards we would run around with the other children from the village while the adults munched on mince pies. We would then have our Christmas dinner and finally be allowed to open our main presents, with the boys falling over themselves and tripping each other up to get to the tree first.

After Dad passed away we found Christmas really hard without him there, and for a few years we didn't stay at home because our grief still felt quite raw. One year we went away skiing and on another occasion we spent Christmas Day in the sun at a resort in the Gambia in Africa – that's the holiday where Paul gave away his new clothes. After that trip, we switched back to celebrating Christmas at home but since I tended to be either studying or working during the holidays, often at night, Christmas didn't seem to hold quite the same importance as it used to.

By the time I turned up on Christmas Day morning in 2009, Mum, David and Paul had already been to church but the four of us gathered round the table and ate a late traditional Christmas lunch with all the trimmings, and then relaxed in front of the TV. Everyone caught up on each other's news while keeping half an eye on the Christmas specials on the box. I crashed out early that night, relieved that I would get more than the six or seven hours' sleep that was becoming the norm with my shifts at the hospital.

Not long after getting up on Boxing Day and sitting around in the kitchen eating breakfast, I needed to make the journey back to Brighton. I had been so looking forward to the Christmas break that I could hardly believe it was over so soon. I felt sad to leave the family after spending such a short amount of time with them. I felt envious of my friends who had the whole week off to relax, catch up on their sleep and spend time with their families, before heading back to work in the new year.

I was due back at the hospital the following day and I was starting to find myself mildly fed up with all the shift work. After the regularity of the nine-to-five days in the GP's surgery, my renal ward hours were quite unsociable, which made it hard to get together with my local friends and enjoy the odd glass of wine on a Saturday. My days off never seemed to coincide with any else's so I often spent them on my own, catching up on chores or wandering into town for

the odd yoga class. I was also finding the hierarchical structure in the hospital difficult and quite stressful. The ward I
was on was consultant-led, because the work I was doing was
so specialized, so I rarely made decisions about patients'
treatments. It was quite different from what I had done before
in the surgery, hearing what was troubling the patients and
working out the best course of treatment. Here, I didn't
manage any patients myself and just followed a lot of instructions, which I found quite disheartening sometimes. I felt so
close to being a fully fledged doctor but this just reminded
me that I still had a way to go.

I had finished my shift on 27 December and I was making the
ten-minute walk home from the hospital, deep in thought
about some of the things I had done that day. One of my
patients' sisters had found out that she was an exact match
and was facing the dilemma of whether to donate her kidney
to her ill brother. She was relatively elderly herself and had
her own health complications, so it wasn't a clear-cut case.
My phone started ringing in my bag and I was so distracted
that for a couple of seconds, I wondered what the noise was.
Snapping back to reality, I fished the phone out of my bag.

I didn't recognize the number but I picked up; I knew it
would be Al because I was expecting his call. I could hear he
was on a train; there was a faint buzz of other people talking
in the background and the soft click of metal on metal as
they commuted home.

'Hi, is that Alison?' he asked. Immediately I was struck by
his strong accent and booming voice, which sounded very

American to me, like someone out of a neon-bright, all-singing, all-dancing Coca-Cola advert.

'Yes,' I replied.

We started talking and my first impressions were that he was loud and confident – for a while I thought he might be a happy-clappy type, who would end up signing off the conversation with a cheery 'Have a nice day!'

He asked about my Christmas: had I had a good time and what had I done? I told him I had been back to Aston Abbotts to spend time with my family and he said he had enjoyed the day with friends in the UK because he didn't have the holiday time off work to head back to Canada. He seemed very interested in my life and asked me lots of questions, in a sort of rapid-fire way: what had I been doing that day? How was I finding my work at the hospital? Did I enjoy it? Where did I live?

When I mentioned that I lived near the seafront in Brighton, strangely, he didn't know where Brighton was, even though I had been told that he had been living in the UK for five years. Registering that I was a bit taken aback by this, he quickly explained that he was living near Croydon and working in London, and had done a fair bit of travelling with his work as an insurance broker for the company LV, but remarked that he hadn't been down to the south coast yet, although he thought it sounded great.

A few minutes into the conversation he said, 'I'm really enjoying talking to you. Would you like to meet up one weekend?'

Aside from his loud voice, I thought he sounded nice too.

He was attentive and seemed really curious about my life, and something inside me was telling me that this could have potential.

'That sounds great,' I replied.

'How about next weekend?' he suggested. 'Are you free Saturday?'

'Yes I am. It's my day off.'

We arranged to meet the following weekend in Leicester Square outside the huge Odeon cinema, and agreed that we should start with a coffee.

'Can I call you again before we meet to chat some more?' he asked.

'Yes, that's fine,' I replied. I thought that seemed like a really respectful gesture because meeting someone who you don't know much about can be awkward and full of stagnant moments and embarrassing pauses. If we spoke again, I knew that by the time we came face-to-face I would know more about him and would feel more at ease.

As promised, he did call a couple of days later and we started to learn more about each other. He asked more about my love of travelling, all about what I had got up to during my twenties, which countries I had lived in and the places in the world that were still on my 'bucket list'. He explained that he was fascinated by history, was wowed by the UK and was doing as much sightseeing as possible in his free time. In some ways he reminded me of James at university, in the sense that he was a bit different from the norm and clearly passionate about what he liked. He didn't care if history might be seen as geeky or boring. I embraced this; I wasn't looking for a vanilla relationship with someone who went to their local pub with their mates every Friday and Saturday night, coming back smelling of kebabs, and whose mum still ironed their shirts. I liked 'different'; after all, I'm not sure I'm your typical girl, either. I'm not crazy about fashion and shopping, I own two pairs of walking boots and only ever wear make-up on special occasions. We ended up talking for the best part of an hour and, despite not having met him yet, I could tell there was a definite spark between us. He sounded like exactly the type of person I'd been hoping to meet – open, passionate about all things and full of life – and as I hung up, a huge smile spread across my face. I was really looking forward to meeting him.

On the Saturday, just a few days into January, I caught the train from Brighton to Victoria and made my way to the Underground, where I was swallowed down into the tunnels with the masses of tourists, like rats into a sewer. It was heaving with people sweating under their thick coats and scarves, and I remembered why I didn't do this journey to London often: I found the enormous crowds suffocating and the constant rush of traffic and noise stifling and oppressive. I was definitely a country girl at heart. It was a hot and uncomfortable journey and, even though it was the weekend, I was sandwiched between an overweight tourist with bad breath and a musty rucksack that was being carried by a girl with thick, ginger dreadlocks, who sighed noisily each time the tube lurched and I was pushed into her.

As I was spat out of the Underground exit onto the pavement and a wave of sharp, cold air whipped me around the face, I didn't feel nervous in the slightest about meeting Al. I knew that we had far more in common than I had had with Frank, and even at this stage I felt pretty certain that we would see each other again. We still hadn't seen pictures of one another because there was a standard no-pictures rule, but I had told him I was 5 foot 6 with dark blonde hair, and that I had a medium build. I had also texted him that morning with details of what I was wearing that day so he could recognize me: I was dressed in blue jeans, boots, a black jacket and a woolly black hat, and I was clutching a shiny patent bag. He told me he was tall, about 6 foot, had dark hair and would also be wearing a black coat.

I arrived a few minutes early and, rather than play it cool and wander around purposely until the allotted hour, I headed straight for the cinema entrance and waited in the outside area of the foyer. Teenagers and tourists milled around me, checking out the times and eye-catching posters of the latest all-action thrillers or romcoms. The buttery smell of popcorn and last night's alcohol lingered as I waited, watching the groups of teenagers sloping past with their trousers slung halfway down their bums, flashing their shiny phones to each other, and the Japanese tourist brigade clicking methodically as they documented their day in photos.

When an Asian man rounded the corner with a big grin on his face, I knew immediately it was Al. He was bang on time. *So far, so good*, I thought.

As he came closer, I noticed that he had a wide, square face, with a well-defined jawline and thick, bushy, inky eyebrows. His eyes were coffee-coloured and almost as dark as his hair, which was cut short and evenly all over. He seemed very self-assured and confident as he made his way towards me, with his head and shoulders held high.

'Hi, Alison?' he said, with a wide, uninhibited smile, all teeth and pink gums.

'Hi, nice to meet you,' I said.

I recall another of my first impressions was that he was dressed very casually, also in jeans and a coat but with a pair of rather blinding, bright white trainers on his feet, which caught me slightly off-guard. I don't know why but I had thought he would be slightly smarter in appearance.

As we settled into initial small talk about our journeys, I can't say I felt the sort of instant physical spark and attraction I had been hoping for, but there was something very charming and charismatic about his personality that kept me interested and I knew I had to move away from thinking about just a physical connection.

'Shall we go and get that coffee?' he said. 'I bet you're freezing. I am.'

We headed off down one of the narrow lanes which snaked away from the central square, and found a quiet coffee shop where Al bought us some drinks and we peeled off our heavy coats and sat down, facing each other.

The questions continued: did I have siblings? When did I decide to become a doctor? What did I love most about my work?

He was animated and attentive, his eyes dancing across my face as I answered. Al told me more about his life growing up.

I only knew that he had lived on the outskirts of the city of Toronto. Quite quickly I learned that he was an only child and had been brought up by his aunt after his parents had died in a car crash when he was young. He didn't seem distressed or troubled when we touched on it, but I presumed it was because the incident had happened when he was so much younger. I thought it best not to probe at this point, so I skirted round the subject then switched the conversation to work. He had already told me he was working as an insurance broker and his office was based in the City. He had worked there for a while and enjoyed it, but I was a bit lost when it came to all things money and finance-related, so didn't ask further about how he had got there or the small details of what he did day-to-day.

Al loved London – I mean, really loved it – and funnily, this made me warm to him. On the weekends he had been checking out all of the main tourist attractions like the Tower of London and the London Dungeon and finding out much more about the capital's rich history. I can't say that history is something I'm particularly enthusiastic about; I enjoy seeing the attractions and spending a few hours milling around places like St Paul's Cathedral or the Natural History Museum, but I'm not so interested in how people lived hundreds or even thousands of years ago. However, history held a certain fascination for Al; he collected knowledge in the way other people might collect stamps or comics, picking up snippets of information here and there and showing them off as and when he could. He kept saying London was 'beautiful' and 'awesome'. I found that, for the first time, I was seeing it from a totally different perspective and I felt really proud of my country. He didn't have a car but held a licence and on a couple of occasions had hired a car to visit different places: once to drive to Windsor to see the castle, and another time he had made the eight-hour car journey to Edinburgh, to explore the historic sites there, including the various castles and abbeys. He was blown away by it, he said, and was planning on returning.

Over an hour and two coffees later, things were going really well. He was so charming and attentive, and his enthusiasm for everything was catching. I could feel myself becoming increasingly captivated by him, and he seemed to like me too as he kept touching my hand as we talked.

'Hey, don't suppose you fancy going to see that new Sherlock Holmes film with Robert Downey Jr and Jude Law?' Al said. 'It's supposed to be good. What do you say?'

He had checked the timetable on his phone while he was on the train on his way to meet me, and had thought that if it went well we could enjoy the afternoon together. I know people say going to the cinema can be quite an awkward thing to do on a first date but he made me feel really at ease and I had no plans.

'Why not? That'd be great. I haven't been to the cinema in ages!'

I hadn't, mainly because it's a particularly coupley thing to do, and I hadn't quite reached the point where I felt entirely comfortable rocking up to see a film on my own.

The auditorium was packed despite the fact that it was mid-afternoon but by then there was none of that uncomfortable sitting-together-but-not-talking feeling that I might have imagined beforehand. We felt relaxed with each other, shared some popcorn and laughed in the same places.

As the credits rolled and we started to file out, exchanging a few words about what we thought of the film – we both agreed it was great – I started to plan my journey home. It was about 6 o'clock and I had no plans that evening so was wondering whether I should get a takeout of sushi, which was one of my favourites, or try one of my Brighton friends on the journey home to see if I could persuade them to come out for a quick drink on the Marina.

As we spilled out of the auditorium, Al asked, 'Do you fancy going to get some dinner?'

I was enjoying his company and the fact he seemed so genuinely interested in what I had to say. *This is turning out to be a really good day*, I thought to myself. It was one of the easiest dates I had ever had.

'Sure,' I replied. 'I'm starving!'

We wound up at a small, independent Italian restaurant nearby where we ate pizzas and talked more about the film, and what we had seen recently; Al was a bit of a film buff and seemed to have an almost exhaustive knowledge of cinema and various actors' roll calls of successes and flops. He talked about how he tracked films in development and found the process of making a big screen blockbuster come to life a riveting subject. He chatted about the early stages of storyboarding, through to set construction and shoots. Again, this isn't something that I have ever spent more than a few minutes really thinking about, but I enjoyed listening to him talk so passionately. This was a guy who knew what he liked, I thought, and what he wanted. He was clearly enjoying London life and the things he was experiencing over here and it was very hard not to let some of his excitement rub off on me, like an invisible cloak of positivity.

We asked for the bill. Al tried to pay but I insisted on going Dutch as I always have.

'I've had a really great day, Alison. Thanks,' he said, as we made our way to the Underground.

'Yes, me too.'

'Would you like to get together again?'

'Yes, I'd like that,' I responded.

Parting ways at the tube station, we hugged goodbye and Al promised to call me. As I descended into the dimly lit underground, I remember thinking to myself that the day had been a successful one; quite simply, I had enjoyed Al's company and I wanted to see him again. OK, so I didn't feel like I wanted to rip his clothes off and dive into bed with him, but maybe a slow-burning passion was what I needed in my life? Maybe if there were a huge spark, the relationship would be full of giddy highs and ridiculous lows. I certainly didn't need that in my life. All the same, there was definitely still something between us, some sort of connection, and I was sure it could be built on over time.

As I strolled home, I watched as Brighton's Saturday night came to life: hen parties squealing, waving their fluffy pink wands and running between bars; mixed groups perching on high stools in wine bars; and students clutching bottles of brightly coloured alcopops overflowing out of the cheap pubs onto the pavements.

Al texted me and I felt a faint buzz of excitement as my phone blinked. He told me he'd had a really good time and asked if I had got home OK, and I replied telling him I was off the train and almost home and that I hoped to see him soon. I felt happy and relaxed. Aside from the fact that I had been flattered by Al's attention, it had been nice just having someone talk to. I had enjoyed doing things that I wouldn't ordinarily do by myself and, as much as I loved Brighton, it had felt good to get away for the day and do something different.

Al was clearly on the same page as me. My phone rang a few days later and he asked if he could he take me for dinner that weekend. He said he would book a restaurant for us, meet me at the station and take us there, and he asked if there was anything that I didn't eat. At Victoria he greeted me with a warm and strong hug, his body solid against mine. He smelt good, of woody cologne, and I noted that he looked smarter because he was wearing a shirt and, thankfully, he had ditched the trainers for a pair of altogether smarter, brown loafer-style shoes.

'It's really good to see you,' he grinned and I smiled back; I felt the same. He was so easy to be around.

We ended up in Queensway, where Al had booked a table at the Royal China, a famous Chinese restaurant. It was definitely a cut above the places I went to with my friends, with stiff napkins and attentive staff hovering nearby. Once again it was really good fun to be with him and the time whizzed past as we shared plates of sesame prawn toast and dim sum. I had that cheerful feeling you get at the start of a relationship that you feel might go somewhere; he was definitely growing on me.

Al never complained about the weather, work or anything in fact; he was always very positive and didn't have a bad word to say about anyone or anything. He stressed again how happy he was to be here in the UK and chatted endlessly about the things he still wanted to see and do. He reminded me of myself when I had been travelling a decade before and the excitement and endless energy I had felt as I carefully plotted my itinerary in Thailand or Japan, making plans to visit different temples or palaces. I might be wrong, but I think that kind of childish eagerness is rare to find in fellow Brits and it was hard not to smile as he rattled off what he had done since we had last seen each other.

He also showed a gentlemanly side and insisted on travelling back with me to Victoria station and, when we parted ways, he kissed me gently for the first time. Fireworks didn't explode inside my head or anything like that, but it felt right as his lips lingered softly on mine for a few seconds.

I felt quietly hopeful that this could be the start of something really special.

Three

The Beginning

As relationships go, this one seemed uncomplicated. Al was open and honest about the fact he liked me; he called like clockwork when he said he would and he always had inventive ideas about what we could get up to on our dates. There was no game-playing or cool silences. We were in contact almost every day, even if it was just a quick text message to say hello and ask each other how our day was going, and we fell into a straightforward routine where we spoke two or three times during the week and saw each other most weekends. Al always sounded delighted to hear from me and I was happy to have someone to talk to and offload about the small stuff that had happened in my life: the consultant whose sharp tone of voice I didn't like; the fact I felt so exhausted after a draining shift; or the plans I had been making to go on a sailing course, just as soon as I could find the time.

I knew Al was keen to take the relationship to the next level because every time we spoke, he casually dropped into the conversation that he wanted to come down to Brighton and see where I lived. When I mentioned a new gastropub that I had been to with some local friends, he remarked, 'That sounds great, we must go there together.' And other times he would say, 'I was reading up about the Royal Pavilion. I would love to see it.' He was hardly subtle, but he was always curious to learn more about my life and I took that to be a really encouraging sign. There is nothing worse than dating someone who is clearly into you on a level of five out of ten, when you are lingering somewhere in the eight out of tens. I liked the fact that he wanted to travel to see me because, in other relationships, I sometimes felt like I was the one permanently coasting along in the middle lane of the motorway on my way to see them.

However, as much as I liked Al and enjoyed spending time with him, initially I was a bit reluctant for him to come to see me in Brighton. I knew if he came down to the south coast he would inevitably stay over at my flat and we would sleep together, and I didn't feel in any rush to take that next step. I enjoyed being on neutral ground and while we met in London we weren't near either of our homes and it was fun to go and see new places and try out different restaurants, without the pressure of what might happen afterwards or whose flat we would be going back to. The more time I spent with Al, the more positive I felt about things between us, but something was holding me back. I still hardly knew him and it just felt right to carry on at a slower pace for a while.

When the agency called following the first couple of dates, enquiring about whether we had got on and what I had thought of Al, I cheerfully told them that the first couple of dates had gone very well, thank you, and that I wasn't interested in meeting anyone else for the time being. While Al and I hadn't discussed exclusivity at that stage, I didn't have the time to see or meet anyone else now and I was happy just to date Al and see him on my free weekends. I didn't feel Al would be going on loads of dates with other women either; he seemed very keen and I could just tell he wasn't the sort of guy who would be running three girlfriends simultaneously while calling them all 'babe'. It just wasn't his style.

For our third date, we met for lunch one weekend at a family-owned Greek restaurant near Green Park, which was one of Al's favourites, and we stuffed ourselves full of tzatziki, fish and Greek salads. A week or so later we got together when I had a day off and we went ice skating at a small rink outside Liverpool Street station one evening, which was still standing – and looking a bit sorry for itself – at the end of January following the festive period. Al had been at one of those 'team-building' days with his work that day, making bread and cakes as part of an exercise, and he came with a large wholemeal loaf as a gift. As we skated around the rink holding on to each other's hands, we cackled with laughter as we narrowly avoided falling over. He was very affectionate and put his arms around my waist and cuddled into me as we whizzed around in circles.

The following week on the phone, he asked me outright, 'So when am I going to be allowed to come and see you in Brighton?'

Eventually, after some persuasion, I agreed to a weekend date on my home turf. I guess by then it felt like the right thing to do, because I had been banging on about how much I loved it there and I wanted to show him my flat and my favourite places in the town.

I timed my invitation to coincide with a few days off I had scheduled after doing a string of night shifts. It also happened to be the time around Valentine's Day and I felt quietly pleased that I would no longer feel like the only singleton on 14 February that year.

'Come this Saturday,' I told him, knowing I would have the Friday off to catch up on my sleep and some of the never-ending admin that seemed to be piling up on my dining-room table.

'Great. I'll book my ticket now,' he said. 'And I'll plan a surprise for us.' I could tell he was trying hard to impress me and keep me interested.

I met him at the station on the Saturday morning and he presented me with a smart box of delicious-looking chocolates.

'These are the brand that makes chocolates for the Queen,' he told me proudly, handing me the pink heart-shaped box of Charbonnel et Walker truffles. 'Happy Valentine's Day.' He kissed me on the cheek and it clicked for the first time that I was in a relationship. My umbrella moment had arrived far quicker than I thought it would.

He had also bought me a card, and luckily I had thought ahead. I had struggled to find one which wasn't filled with ruby red hearts and declarations of love. I quite enjoy making cards, although I don't have time do it often, so in the end I made a fairly plain but thoughtful one for him.

'I've organized something special for us to do today,' he said, beaming, as he took my hand and we left the station, heading down the hill in the direction of the seafront.

had complained to him that week that during the previ-
s year I had signed myself up to a number of sailing
urses and organized the time off work so I could go, which
was never easy, with rotas and shifts to account for. Every time, the dreadful British weather had meant the course was cancelled at the last minute.

As a surprise, Al had organized a private boat trip from Brighton Marina with just a skipper at the helm and us on board. It was a bitterly cold day and the sky was thick with slate grey cloud, but we had fun. We skirted the Sussex coast towards Newhaven and the view from the water was mainly just white cliffs but it was a novelty to be out on the sea and it was a really thoughtful gesture that Al had made – no one had done anything like that for me in a long time.

For lunch, I took him to Bill's cafe in The Lanes, a venue that I love because it always feels a bit special, with deli-style food and cosy seating and homemade condiments stacked on wooden shelves on the walls. Afterwards, we wandered around the narrow and twisting alleys, checking out the little independent shops selling pretty jewellery, dusty antiques and vintage clothing. As we passed a health food shop selling wheatgrass juice, I insisted we stop for a couple of shots as I had heard it had revitalizing properties.

'Yuk!' I declared, nearly spitting it out again as I munched on half a strawberry, which is supposed to sweeten the after-taste.

'What do you mean, yuk? It's delicious!'

I don't know what planet Al was on that day as I've never tasted anything quite so disgusting!

Late in the afternoon we headed back to my flat. The pl was quite quirky and I had often wondered whether it use be old servants' quarters, because the landlord lived at t. end of the long driveway in a very imposing whitewashed house and there were two or three flats like mine at the start of the driveway. When I had quizzed him he had told me it was once a farm and my flat had been where the cows had lived. Whatever the truth of the matter, I liked to indulge my idea that people serving the main house hundreds of years ago, like *Downton Abbey*'s Mrs Patmore or Anna and Mr Bates, once lived there in modest lodgings with open fires and simple comforts.

It was a ground-floor studio and I shared an entrance with the flat upstairs, which mirrored mine. The flat was L-shaped: as you walked in, the small dining area was on the left where I had a table and chairs, and behind it I had a sofa and TV and then my bed and my wardrobe. One of the flat's best features was its two huge bay windows that meant it was always light and had a spacious feel, despite the fact it was small. Round the corner of the 'L', there was a kitchen and a long corridor leading off through to the bathroom. When I had moved in, I had filled it with a mixture of furniture that I found in Brighton's best second-hand shops and a few bits from IKEA. I had made it feel homely with pictures on the walls and photographs dotted around the place from my various travels. Outside, it had its own shared garden and, best of all, it was located just two roads back from the seafront, so I tried to stroll out to the sea every day. It was also the perfect location for work as it was a short ten-minute walk to Brighton's main hospital, where I was doing most of my training. After a somewhat nomadic existence before moving to Brighton, I finally felt like I had put down some solid roots and this flat was a large part of that.

Al cooked some dinner for us – I seem to recall tha⌐ something simple like a vegetable stir-fry – and ⌐en we snuggled up on the sofa to watch a DVD. This was my idea of the perfect Saturday; Al was clearly as uninterested in going to a busy bar or club as I was, and I felt really relaxed.

That night we slept together for the first time. It wasn't amazing and again, there were no fireworks, but it felt right and I was completely at ease. Afterwards we cuddled for a while and we both fell into a deep sleep.

We woke up late and had another lazy day. After breakfast and mugs of steaming coffee, we walked around the park, which was located just behind where I lived. It was just a green field and not particularly exciting but while my choice would be to walk to the sea, Al liked it there because it was deserted, except for the odd dog walker or jogger. We were having fun together and enjoying each other's company, but I itched to leave the park and be by the sea instead – whenever I had a free moment I tried to spend it there.

I stopped for a moment and said, 'Why don't we head

towards the front for a bit? Don't you want to make the most of being near the sea before you head back to London?'

He stepped towards me and circled his arms around me with a mischievous grin on his face. 'I want to stay right here. Why would I want to take you somewhere full of other people when I could keep you here and have you all to myself?'

I smiled as we carried on walking.

On our return, we watched another DVD from my collection of action movies, murder mysteries and a few romcoms, and ate lunch together. As Al left, he told me he loved spending time with me. He said I was his perfect woman, and I felt flattered, happy and excited about where this new relationship might be heading.

After the first weekend Al stayed over, the romance moved up a gear pretty quickly. Al suggested that he come down to see me again the next weekend and I was happy to not trek into London and navigate the tubes as I was still working very long shifts on the renal ward. Slowly but surely we slotted into a pattern of me coming home on a Friday exhausted from my week and diving into bed, often without bothering with dinner because I was so shattered. Al would arrive by train on the Saturday morning and we would head out of town in my car. We had talked about checking out some of the local places, so we went on long walks at some of the nearby National Trust properties, where I had a membership, and on another occasion I drove us up to Ashdown Forest. While we were there Al organized for us to go pony trekking, which was something he said he had done before and loved. We donned hard, musty-smelling hats and went down the local bridle paths, Al clinging on to the pommel of the saddle, while I teased him saying I thought he was an expert. Another weekend, we headed across to the Isle of Wight by ferry and ate dinner on the seafront, then spent the night in a quaint hotel. As well as doing lots of outdoorsy things to please me, Al was also very interested in castles, so we spent two different weekends exploring Leeds Castle and then Arundel Castle.

I liked the fact we were getting out and about and Al was always attentive and caring, cooking dinner most evenings after our travels and making small gestures, like buying me pretty bunches of flowers or boxes of chocolates. Sometimes we'd go out in the evenings for dinner or for a drink at one of the bars or pubs on the seafront.

Al remembered everything I told him and questioned me closely about my week, and he really listened to what I said; he made me feel like nothing was more important than me. The more time I spent with him the happier I was that he had come into my life, although I still wasn't sure if it was serious and I hadn't thought about whether I wanted this to be a long-term thing. Looking back, sometimes it's hard to see that time with a clear perspective, but I remember feeling excited about seeing him every weekend and enjoying making plans and thinking of the places we could go together. Before Al was my boyfriend, my free time had been spent locally with friends and at the odd yoga class but now I had plans and was venturing out of Brighton to see different places, which I liked. My life had changed for the better since meeting him.

At the beginning of April, I switched from the renal ward to a placement in the A&E department. I knew it would be a job that I either loved or hated. Most of my fellow trainees relished their time there, saying it was the first time they felt like a 'proper' doctor, making instant decisions and deciding on treatment, but they also confessed that the one thing that they hated were the hours because their shifts were long, stressful and irregular. You came out the other side of this particular placement a broken person, they said. I knew that I would be on early shifts following late shifts, day shifts following a row of nights and I would be lucky to ever have two consecutive days off. Everyone said that a couple of months into it and they felt they needed a year – or a very long and luxurious holiday – to recover from the way the weird timings had shifted their body's equilibrium.

However, the variety was exciting and in my eyes this was what medicine was all about and I was really looking forward to it. I knew by that point that 'generalist' medicine, where you see a bit of everything in the space of a few hours, was what I wanted to do long-term, so my future when I finally finished all my training would be either in a busy GP's surgery or in an altogether more hectic and chaotic A&E department. Along with butterflies and excitement, I was also nervous; I knew many people who turned up would be very sick or in a lot of pain, and I wondered whether I would be able to respond fast enough and make those razor-sharp decisions that sometimes saved lives. I would need to be on the ball, big time. However, I was up for the challenge and couldn't wait to get started.

Given the new rota and lack of predictability, I knew I would struggle to find time to see Al, because I only had one weekend off every two months and the odd day here and there, and with Al working nine to five Monday to Friday at LV, our timetables were seriously out of synch. It soon became clear that this was a big issue, especially for him. By then we had been dating for three months but had seen each other most weekends since his initial trip to Brighton.

'When are we going to see each other next?' Al demanded after I told him I wouldn't have a weekend free for at least six weeks. 'I want to spend more time with you.'

I didn't have an answer for him but I don't remember feeling desperately upset about it or annoyed that I was going to have to sacrifice time with him for work; it was still early days and while I liked him and enjoyed his company, I wasn't sure what the future held for us. My job had to come first.

'I have to do this job and I want to do A&E,' I replied. 'My training is my priority. I have no say over when my shifts are. It's completely out of my hands when I have time off.'

'We could think about living together,' he suggested, not looking me straight in the face. 'I'd like that. We know already we get on really well. We could rent somewhere new together and set ourselves up properly.'

'No Al,' I told him. 'It's far too soon. I don't want that yet.'

I was surprised he had suggested something so permanent after such a short time together but tried not to let the shock show on my face.

'But it wouldn't be that different from how it is already,' he argued.

'No. I don't feel ready for that.'

I was quite adamant that living together was still not on the agenda in my eyes, but Al wasn't easily put off. In a way I felt quietly flattered because I was left in no doubt how he felt about me, but I still didn't feel ready to make that kind of commitment. I had never lived with anyone before, so wanted it to feel right when I finally did take the plunge. I imagined moving into a new house with a boyfriend and picking out furniture together, setting up home together, not someone squeezing into my small flat.

'OK, I could come down and spend a few days with you during the week and commute into work from Brighton. I don't mind doing the train journey. In fact, it gives me time to relax or catch up on some reading.'

This seemed like a far better solution.

'Really? I won't be around much, but if you really want to, that's fine by me,' I conceded. 'It'll be nice to have a couple of hours in the evenings once or twice a week, I guess.'

I liked having Al around and felt that if he wanted to make the three-hour round journey a couple of days during the week so we could see each other, then that worked for me. I knew his job was less stressful than mine and desk-based, so was relieved to have found a resolution that didn't involve him moving himself in. I gave him a spare set of keys, which he happily put into his pocket.

The following Saturday morning, Al turned up with a couple of dark-coloured holdalls and a rucksack.

'Just a few things – my clothes, toothbrush and a few other bits,' he said, stashing them in the corner of my dining area. I didn't really think twice about it. After all, he was going to start staying a few nights a week, so would need to have some of his belongings with him.

As my placement at A&E started, I would often return in the evenings to find Al cooking dinners, like salads or pasta for us to share. The flat would be spotless, my washing would be hanging up and drying in the corner and he would have my favourite jazz music playing on the CD player. Even though he was spending more time at my flat, on some days I still didn't see him at all because I was working nights or split shifts and would be at home during the day when Al was at work. He would leave me lovely notes and letters when he went to work and tell me how much he missed me and that he had filled the fridge with my favourite foods.

On my days off I spent most of the time in bed trying to catch up on my sleep and readjust my body clock, which felt all over the place. Some days I felt seasick and disorientated because my body was so out of synch. I was starting to find that I was eating at weird times, was getting far less sleep than was ideal and that sometimes days blurred into nights and then into weeks. Sometimes my head felt furry from lack of sleep and unless I was at work and forcing myself to fire on all cylinders and exist on adrenaline, then I just seemed to almost float through my free time, my eyes gritty from tiredness and my limbs floppy, like a ragdoll.

Inevitably, my social life also started to drop off because I was working such unsociable hours. Unwittingly I was becoming more and more reclusive but it was very much through the circumstance of work, rather than choice, at that time. A couple of close friends who I regularly went to yoga with in Brighton had nine to five jobs and had both fallen into serious relationships around the same time that I had met Al, so we naturally saw each other less. On a couple of occasions when I did go for a drink with friends, Al came too and seemed to get on well with everyone. He asked lots of questions, laughed in all the right places and bought rounds of drinks.

I only see my two best friends from university, who live in Leeds and Shropshire, once or twice a year, and I send them birthday and Christmas cards, but I'm not the sort of girl who has someone she calls every day for advice, gossip or help with life's big questions. I'm so used to keeping my own counsel because I travelled so much in my twenties. And anyway, some evenings I found myself too worn out to pick up the phone and was very happy just to eat something Al had cooked before flopping into bed to try and catch up on what seemed like a deficit of months' worth of sleep.

When we had the odd weekend off together Al and I still made the most of our time together and he happily planned things for us to do. One weekend we went down to the New Forest and went kayaking together on the Beaulieu River. It was a beautiful late spring day and the water twinkled in the sun. The surface of the river was teaming with hundreds of jellyfish, which bobbed along with the ebb and flow of the water. On another occasion he organized for us to do a 'Learn to Tango and Salsa' course across a weekend at one of the professional dance studios in the centre of Brighton. We tried our best but we were both rubbish, and spent as much time laughing at ourselves as we did trying to pick up the various Latin rhythms and moves.

Throughout all this time, Al carried his camera everywhere and always took photos, or asked someone else to take photos of us together. Like most people, I don't really like having my picture taken, but after a while I got used to it and put Al's fondness for taking pictures down to him being a tourist and wanting to document his time in the UK.

In May, Al had booked to go home to Canada to stay with his Aunt Gulshan. He said he wanted to catch up with some old friends, sort out some paperwork and bring some more belongings back with him, like an expensive formal suit he had there. I had overheard him talking to his aunt regularly on the phone and they talked easily about their work and respective lives. Sometimes they spoke to one another in a different language, which sounded like it could be Urdu or Hindi but I knew it was one of the lesser-spoken Indian dialects. Al said they were close because she had brought him up since the age of three when the car crash had happened. I never quizzed him too much about the actual accident where he lost his parents. After losing Dad, I knew how painful it would be for him to have to talk about it. I felt he would tell me in his own time exactly how his early years had unfolded and how he felt about it. However, whenever it did crop up in conversation, any comment he made about it would be brief and emotionless. Perhaps, I reasoned, he couldn't remember much about that time and never knew anything different and had accepted his lot in life.

As Al travelled back and forth between his Croydon flat, his office in the City and Brighton, slowly his possessions started to mount up in my flat. I had allocated him a corner near the dining room table and the space around it, which I didn't use. A drawer clearly wouldn't suffice in this case.

The weekend before he went on his trip, he arrived with another two dark grey holdalls, which he piled on top of the rest of his belongings, like some sort of luggage rack. These final bags were just enough to tip the balance and make me feel slightly uncomfortable about him invading my personal space.

'You've got loads of bags here,' I said one day. 'What on earth have you got in there? The kitchen sink?'

'It's just a few bits and bobs. I'll tidy them up more,' he replied as he started stacking the bags carefully on top of each other. I hoped that perhaps he would take some of it away with him when he left for Canada.

With hindsight, I can see how little I knew about his life before he came to the UK. He often talked about friends in Canada: a Greek friend who cooked a mean kleftiko, someone who had followed the same path as me to Asia and taught English in Japan for a few years, and another guy who had worked his way up the ranks at PayPal and was now one of the directors there, but it was hard for me to find out more about Al because he hadn't grown up here. He was very eager to share what he could of his life here, however. One evening when I had a rare day off I went to meet him from work so we could go out for dinner in London at a lovely little bistro around the corner from his office. He took me up into his workplace, which was in a very impressive office – at least to me being used to greying, grotty, often smelly hospitals. I made small talk with a few female colleagues while he finished up something at his desk and they seemed friendly, asking me about what I did and my life in Brighton. Al quickly finished up and we went off on our way.

The one question I always get now after everything that happened was whether there were any warning signs but I can honestly say I don't think there were then. He seemed to live a very normal life and I perhaps was blinded by those feelings of tenderness and warmth that you get when you are in a new relationship.

One day around this time Al told me he loved me for the first time. It was a beautiful spring day and the sun was high in the sky, so we decided to go for a walk along the beach. The seafront has never lost its magic for me, even now. I could never tire of the salty scent that lingers in my hair for a couple of hours afterwards or the feeling of wonder I get looking out into the distance over the crashing waves. As he uttered those three words, I still wasn't sure if I loved him back. Of course I liked him a lot but didn't want to say it for the sake of it – or return the compliment just to make him happy. I knew I had to mean it, so instead I just squeezed his warm hand and kissed his stubbly cheek. I hoped the time would come when I would be able to say it back to him, and feel that depth of feeling from the tips of my toes, through to the pit of my stomach. I wanted that time to come more than anything; it just hadn't arrived yet.

Being on the ball and making crucial decisions was so important in the A&E department that I poured all of my energy into it. I wanted to be good at it and impress my colleagues and, as I had imagined beforehand, it was proving to be the exciting placement that I knew it would be.

We saw a bit of everything, from adults with unexplained chest pain or breathlessness to the same drunk crazies that rocked up every Saturday night at 11 p.m., who would be placed on a trolley in the corridor or up against the wall and prodded every once in a while to make sure they were still breathing and sleeping the alcohol off. I learnt a lot from the nurses who had been there for years; most of them had a very dry sense of humour and knew exactly who to look out for. Initially I was shocked when they told people in no uncertain terms to get out and stop wasting their time. I was pretty sure it was our job to help them, but soon I realized that, like some sort of local pub, there were always the 'regulars' demanding something that would never help their cause in the long-term. Along with the drunks, there were the druggies who would regularly roll up and ask for a hit of whatever they were addicted to and had to be marched off the premises, or the people that would beg to be admitted to one of the wards because they were suicidal, even though for many it was often just a cry for attention and a stay in hospital wouldn't have been the right thing for them. Weekend nights also saw the 'party crew': the people who had overdosed on recreational drugs or stacked it on the dance-floor during some serious dance-offs and banged their heads or sprained their ankles. Sunday brought with it members of local rugby and football teams, splattered in mud, clutching dodgy looking arms or wonky shoulders which had popped out of their sockets during a scrum or nasty tackle. It was constantly demanding but always exciting.

To help me and the other registrars cope with everything we saw on A&E, Wednesday afternoons would be dedicated to teaching, and the local GPs covered the department while we learned all sorts of practical things, like dealing promptly with anaphylactic shock, suturing surface wounds and how to deal with dislocations. It was very hands-on and the consultants were extremely approachable. Everybody had to muck in because it was so busy and demanding, so it didn't feel like there was this big pecking order, where I was scrambling along the bottom. I was always able to find a friendly senior face to answer my queries if I was ever unsure of anything and needed reassurance about a decision I had made. As well as working out of the main hospital in Brighton, I also did a number of shifts at the Princess Royal Hospital in Haywards Heath, where I would be the only doctor on call during some nights, which was as testing as it was plain terrifying.

Even though there was a lot of shift work, I liked seeing

the same familiar faces every day; the same raised eyebrows from the nurses or calm, bespectacled grins from the doctors. I found that I was starting to get to know other teams in different departments of the hospital, like gynaecology, paediatrics, orthopaedics, surgery and of course, the paramedics, who raced in with the emergencies and passed over the details they had. A&E felt like the beating heart of a far bigger body and it was a real insight into how a hospital functioned as a whole. I felt as though the staff I saw every day were becoming like my surrogate family of wise aunts and knowledgeable grandparents. Some days, when I was rushed off my feet and felt I could cry with exhaustion, or I faced rude or argumentative people at 3 o'clock in the morning who I was trying to help, it was my colleagues who kept me going and pulled me through with a cup of tea, a biscuit and a friendly chat. When I mentioned this to one of my favourite nurses one day, she agreed that it was the staff and sense of camaraderie they shared that had kept her on the hospital's payroll for over thirty years.

I was so immersed in life in A&E that the week Al was away in Canada seemed to fly by. When he returned he came straight back to my flat from the airport, rather than go to his own first, and he was carrying even more things with him. When I got back from work that night and clocked the huge mound of possessions, I knew I needed to say something about it. I was aware that he'd brought things back on the plane with him but I couldn't understand why they were at my home rather than at his flat. Like a lot of people I avoid confrontation at any cost and inwardly squirm at the thought of an argument, but as happy as I was to see him after his time away, I knew I needed to ask him exactly what was going on. I had an unnerving feeling that, despite what we had spoken about, he was slowly moving himself in against my wishes.

'Have you moved in?' I asked outright, when a good moment presented itself over dinner a day or so after his return. 'You've got quite a lot of stuff here now.'

'Oh no, no, I haven't. I know it looks like a lot,' he said, glancing quickly at the pile in the room. 'I'll take a few things back to my flat if you like? I came straight to see you because I've missed you. I missed you loads and loads and thought about you every day. Have you missed me? Bet you've missed my cooking?'

I immediately relaxed. *I was just reading too much into a perfectly innocent situation*, I said to myself.

'Of course I missed you,' I said, smiling across the table at him. 'It felt strange without you here. I've got used to you being around.'

While we were eating, I suggested we buy a hanging rail for some of his work clothes that he had laid out over the top of everything, so when he was staying with me he didn't arrive at work looking all crumpled. After a trip to B&Q, he hung up a couple of suits and shirts but the five or six holdalls stayed spilling out of the corner and around the table. Bizarrely, some of the bags had padlocks on them and there was also some diving gear, including some large blue flippers and a snorkel, and I couldn't work out quite how they had arrived at my flat or if he planned to go diving off the Brighton coast, but I hoped they would disappear soon.

Two weeks later Al still hadn't moved anything out and had spent every day and night at the flat since our chat, and I was growing increasingly confused. Part of me rationalized that if he had moved in completely, he would have had a lot more possessions with him, such as kitchen utensils and maybe even some furniture, like the odd mirror or IKEA bookshelf, the sort of things I had gathered during my lifetime. But I knew I had to ask him yet a second time, just to put my uneasy mind at rest.

Again it was over dinner one day that I approached the subject.

'Al. You haven't been home for ages. Are you sure you haven't moved in?'

There was a moment's pause before he said, somewhat sheepishly, 'Well, I had to let my flat go. I've been meaning to talk to you about it. My contract was up for renewal and I'm spending so much time here it didn't make sense to sign up for another year.'

My cheeks started to burn. I was really angry and annoyed. 'Al, don't you think we should have had a conversation about it first?' I demanded.

'I know but it just happened. I thought we would be living together before too long anyway. It makes sense.'

'That wasn't the agreement,' I said, trying not to raise my voice. 'I told you I wasn't ready to live together. If you were going to let your contract go, we should've had a conversation about it first.'

Aside from the fact we hadn't discussed it, I didn't feel my flat was big enough for two people. It's the sort of place that an estate agent would describe as 'cosy' at best.

'I'm sorry, I thought you wouldn't mind,' he said, coming over to hug me. 'I love being here with you. I want to look after you. We've been spending so much time together that I thought it would make sense. I know I should've talked to you first but it all happened very quickly.'

It was the first time we had exchanged cross words. I was flattered by his enthusiasm for our relationship but at the same time I felt quite uncomfortable and hopeless, a bit like a raft being swept along by a more determined force. However, I cooled down quickly. I'm always told I'm a practical person, and able to brush over the emotional side of things. And that's exactly what I did then, sweeping up my doubts and parking them firmly in the corner of my mind. I decided that if he had let his flat go, then there was nothing that I could do about it, not now anyway, and maybe we needed to think seriously about finding a more spacious home for us to share when my flat came up for renewal the following August.

My other worry was about friends or family coming to stay, which did happen on the odd occasion. Previously they had always bunked down on a blow-up bed in the bedroom, but with Al sharing, this wasn't possible without being plain weird.

'I'll stay in a B&B nearby,' he said. 'Don't worry about that.

I'll move out for the night or even a few nights if you want people here.'

'OK,' I responded.

We also had to talk about money because I felt he needed to contribute towards my rent. I was aware he earned good money with work so I knew it wouldn't be an issue for him to pay his way. We often split bills for meals and so forth when we went out, but now we would need to formalize our living costs. Again, Al didn't complain and bent over backwards to reassure me that everything would be fine. He could clearly tell that I was angry but ultimately he had got what he wanted.

I never really thought my first experience of living with someone would be like this but things never quite go to plan, do they? I concluded that Al had simply arrived faster than me at that point where he was ready to take that next step and it would work out fine in the end.

'I love you, Alison. Everything about you,' he said, trying to hug me. 'Your smile, your laugh, your eyes; please don't be angry with me.'

'Please talk to me first before you make decisions like this by yourself,' I replied.

I hoped that this would be the first and last time Al took huge decisions like this into his own hands.

Four

Meeting the Family

June 2010 heralded the month in which my mum would finally marry her long-term partner David Gray. David had separated from his first wife in 1981 and had finally got divorced in 2002. Mum and David met in 1998 in a chance encounter in a pub, where they had both been taken by friends in an attempt to encourage them to 'get a life', and since that first 'hello', they hadn't looked back. After about five years together they knew they wanted to get married but decided to wait until we were all settled in our respective lives with homes and jobs. They had finally got round to organizing the day to make it official that year and had planned a ceremony at the local church, followed by cream teas back at home in the garden, then a reception for family and close friends at a venue nearby afterwards. All the Hewitt children get on well with David and after Dad's death I was happy to see Mum with someone who brought back the old sparkle in her, who made her happy. They are like two peas in a pod these days.

Mum didn't want a big hen do before the Big Day, claiming it's not quite the same the second time round, but as part of the celebrations we organized a night away at a spa called Whittlebury Hall in Northamptonshire for the two of us during the first weekend of the month. In honour of Mum's impending nuptials, we were upgraded to an incredibly grand room which was far bigger than we needed, and we spent the first day testing out the huge swimming pool and various heat rooms, like the sauna, steam room and cold experiences, gingerly entering the ice cave or throwing ice all over ourselves from a bucket in the ice room. I treated myself to a much-needed full body massage, where the lady pummelled by achy back, and Mum and I did a Pilates session together on the Sunday morning.

I had already told her about Al on the phone but on the Saturday evening, when we sat down to a three-course meal, I filled her in on what had happened since we last spoke about him.

'Al has moved in,' I told her. 'We never really talked about it but he gave up his flat.'

'How do you feel about that?' she asked, remaining neutral.

'I'm not totally convinced,' I said, feeling strangely emotional. 'I like him but I'm not sure he's "The One". I'm not sure he's not, I just don't know yet. I do like him but I've been a bit thrown by what has happened.'

'Well, just be careful and see how it goes. He should've asked before he moved himself in, Alison. That's not how these things normally happen. It's a big step and you should both have agreed on it beforehand.'

I knew she was right. Suddenly I wanted to cry. I think I had bottled up how I really felt about it and had tried to just shrug off any uncomfortable feelings. It was like she was the voice inside my head, echoing back my own thoughts and feelings.

'I know,' I said, swallowing hard.

'And is it really big enough for you both?'

'Not really. That's another thing that's making me unsure about the whole situation. He's said he'll move out to a B&B when I have people to stay so at least that's something . . .' I trailed off.

I managed to suppress the tears that were close to the surface and buoyed myself up instead, not wanting to ruin the lovely day I'd been having with Mum. I decided there was no point worrying about 'what ifs'. *If it works out, great,* I told myself, *and if it doesn't, then it doesn't. It's as simple as that.*

Gearing up to the wedding day itself, Al kept saying he really wanted to come with me as my guest. For a while I agonized over the decision because it would mean him meeting every single member of my family and all our close friends in one hit and I thought it would be quite daunting for him. Dave was flying over from Australia, as were Mark and his family from Norway, and David's son Ollie along with his wife, Sarah, and two sons, who lived in New York, were also jetting in to celebrate. It wasn't a big wedding but I was also unsure about bringing him along as my 'other half', because it suggested the romance was more mature than I felt it was at that stage. One thing I dreaded was being asked by well-meaning villagers when Al was going to 'pop the question' and being told that, back in their day, a woman would have had three children by the age of twenty-five. I was also acting as a bridesmaid on the day, so would have no time to introduce Al to the other guests and look after him, and I had been so busy with work that there hadn't even been the time to introduce him to Mum and David beforehand. In my mind it would be every new partner's nightmare to be introduced to the family on this kind of scale but Al was persistent. It was only with a week or so to go that I made the decision that, if he really wanted to come, then I would make the necessary phone call home to ask if it would be OK to add an extra person to the ever-growing invite list.

Mum and David were happy for Al to come along and were eager to meet him, but we decided that we needed something for him to do on the day, so we charged him with looking after my gran, Peggy Hewitt. Still fit and bright as a button at eighty-six, she was married to my grandfather on my dad's side, after he had left his first wife. With no kids of her own, she has always taken a keen interest in all of us and as children we often went to stay with her at her home in Sutton Coldfield in the Midlands during our holidays or on the odd weekend. She has never been your typical gran, banging on about 'the youth of today' while waving a walking stick around – far from it, in fact; she has always been very young at heart. She was really interested in our hobbies and loved taking my brothers to skateboarding parks when they were young, where she would cheer them on. On other occasions she took us to musicals at the theatre or to the local park for a game of football or rounders, and we always felt like she really enjoyed our company. As she's got older, she's quite right wing in her opinions, but in a good way. She's very matter of fact and calls a spade a spade, and we love her to pieces. We decided that matching her and Al up would be the perfect compromise, asking him to look after her and vice versa, as both of them would feel like they were helping with something on the day and had a special 'job' to do.

The week before the wedding my brother Dave paid a brief visit on one of his whirlwind tours that he always made when he came over, packing in roughly twenty friends and all his siblings in about three days before he headed back to Sydney. We had always been very close and Al was keen to meet him and bought him an expensive bottle of wine, which I felt was a lovely gesture. Dave only stopped at the flat for a couple of hours – a lot of which he spent diverting phone calls from his friends who were planning a big night out – but during that time Al stuck close to me, like glue, and was very attentive. I felt that maybe he was feeling a bit anxious and insecure about making a good impression and didn't think anything more of it, although in hindsight I think this was him show-ing the first signs of wanting to have me all to himself and not 'share' me with anyone.

I worked right up until the night before the wedding and it was all a bit of a last-minute, crazy rush making it back to Aston Abbotts in time. I had struggled to find a bridesmaid dress that was not too girly and was the right shade of pink to match my mum's frock, and it was only about a week before that I had located one in the right size and we drove home via

Basingstoke to pick it up. I was frazzled and stressed and, as much as I was looking forward to the day, I can't say I was in exactly the right frame of mind after a few long and difficult shifts in the A&E department.

By the time we pulled into the driveway of my mum's house it was late on the Friday evening and, in contrast to the quiet of the village, lights poured out from every window and noise seeped through the old brick walls.

Mum and David had already left and were staying at Hart-well House, an impressive Grade I-listed stately home not that far away, which they had chosen to host their wedding reception. Even without them there, it was a full house split-ting at the seams, with every bedroom full of suitcases, dresses and suits hanging over doors and small children run-ning around screeching from overtiredness and excitement. I think Mum and David had strategically planned to get away to avoid some of the chaos. Downstairs the adults were rush-ing around, trying to organize baths for the children and then get them into bed, while also making the preparations for the day ahead.

Even though Mum and David had asked for no wedding gifts and had said that if people really wanted to make a ges-ture then they could make a donation to Oxfam, Al left an expensive bottle of Moet champagne as a present on the kitchen table. He also bought my brothers gifts and a book for my gran. I didn't think anything of this and found it quite endearing that he was trying so hard to make a good impres-sion. Everyone likes a surprise gift, don't they? I don't think I was worried about what people thought about Al at the time;

I was more concerned about how he felt, because for much of the time I left him on his own while I chatted to my brothers, my gran and David's son and his wife, and tried to make myself useful. At the same time, I was exhausted and didn't really feel prepared for the day ahead.

There was no time to sit back and relax the following morning and after a hasty breakfast I dashed off to the hairdresser's to get my hair done and then back home to get myself together.

The day itself was a happy blur. Mum looked radiant and David looked like the cat that had got the cream as they said their vows at the church, St James the Great, in front of all their friends and family and a lot of people from the village, who huddled together in groups. As the vicar announced that they were husband and wife, a big cheer went up.

After the ceremony, we walked back to the house to the sound of the church bells ringing in the background, where we served cream teas in our garden for all our village friends, our close family friends and the family itself. I remember spending a lot of time in the kitchen refreshing teapots, sending out more scones and serving drinks, making sure everyone had a full glass or cup. I wanted everything to be perfect for Mum, who had toiled away for us over the years. She was – and still is – the real backbone of the family.

When I glanced around to see if Al was managing, I glimpsed him standing with my gran in the kitchen and a bit later I saw him speaking to my Aunty Irene in the garden. As I poured water into the kettle and flicked the boil switch for yet more teas, one of my mum's friends was clearing up on the work surface near me.

'He's doing quite well out there,' she remarked. 'It must be pretty daunting for him.'

'Yes, you would think so but he was determined to come.'

'Good for him,' she said. 'It's really nice to meet him. He seems like a lovely chap. He's very confident and charming.'

Al seems to be doing OK, I thought. After the tea, all the family and some close friends travelled over to Hartwell House by car, where we were served a three-course meal and there were a few traditional speeches, including ones from David and his best man. I sat on the top table and Al was placed next to me. Al was very affectionate that afternoon and was constantly placing a hand on my leg, a palm around my waist, or a protective arm around my shoulder. I took this as a sign that he was just a bit insecure or overwhelmed, and needed some reassurance, but when he lingered a bit too long, I carefully untangled myself from him and would give his hand or leg an encouraging squeeze.

The reception didn't go on late and we headed back to Aston Abbotts where we excused ourselves as soon as it was politely acceptable. As I climbed into bed, Al reached over and whispered, 'Can I have a cuddle?'

'Al, I'm knackered and you get to cuddle me all the time,' I replied as exhaustion washed over me. 'Are you OK?'

'I'm fine. I just feel like I've barely seen you today.'

'I know,' I said, shutting my eyes. 'You know what these family events are like.' I crashed out about three seconds later.

*

Afterwards, as I had guessed, all the family and friends wanted to discuss what they thought of my new boyfriend. I later discovered that apparently the feedback from relatives and friends to Mum and David was that Al was 'charming, if a little intense'. Most people commented on how sad it was that he had lost his parents at such a young age in such horrible circumstances, so it had obviously been a key topic of conversation on the day, and afterwards Mum remarked on how keen Al had been to tell her that he was an orphan.

However, what I didn't learn until much later was that my gran wasn't such a fan. She had told Mum that she thought he was evasive and was 'hiding something'. In the way that only older people can, during their time together she had clearly interrogated him about the past in an unassuming, forthright way. Although he had been consistent but economical with the details about his childhood and the fact he was an orphan, when my gran had probed further, like some sort of Miss Marple on the quest for the truth, she hadn't managed to uncover as much as she had wanted. She thought he must have 'a big secret', she said. Maybe he could have a wife or even children back in Canada? Maybe he was leading some sort of double life? Whatever it was, she remarked, there was something he wasn't telling me and she was insistent that 'this is not the man for Alison', repeating this statement to Mum and David at least three times.

'He's not right for her,' she said. 'I just know it.'

Al and I headed straight back to Brighton the morning after the wedding because I had a late shift that day, and I was straight back into work mode as we sped up the motorway. Al buzzed with tales from the day and how much he liked my family. I imagined my big family was the sort of household he would have dreamt of as he grew up an only child. He loved seeing a traditional English wedding, he raved, and he could picture my life more clearly having met all the people I had talked about. He thought my brothers were great guys and he had enjoyed meeting David's son, Ollie, and his wife.

Mum and David had decided that because all the family had come over for the Big Day, they would delay their honeymoon to Sicily until later in the year. They were also busy because David had kept the house he had lived in during his bachelor years in Bedfordshire and was in the process of moving into the family home, with a lot of his personal clutter.

The following Friday I had a day off from work, so Mum planned to bring my eldest nephew, Ben, who was just four years old at the time, down to Brighton. Al booked a B&B for them to stay in, telling me it would be far more comfortable than a night on the hard floor or the blow-up bed. Again I didn't think twice about the fact he had agreed before that he would move out if family or friends wanted to stay, and Al even offered to pay for it. In the end, he reserved a room but I picked up the bill. I didn't mention it to Mum because I didn't think she needed to know the details. Also, I didn't feel like explaining myself again, so just didn't make a drama out of it.

After they arrived, Mum, Ben, Al and I went out to the seafront on the Thursday and had an early dinner, where we shared mezze and Ben ate chips at a smart restaurant on the seafront, called Alfresco. It was the first time that Mum was able to have a proper chat with Al, so was able to ask him more about his life and family. Mum asked him sensitively about his parents and what had happened and Al went into a long, convoluted story about how much he remembered about the crash where he had been thrown through the windscreen. He said he had vivid recollections of sounds of his parents screaming for help, the smell of burning petrol and images of flames as the car burned. I think Mum was quite taken aback by how candidly he talked about it, and was surprised by his lack of emotion, as I had been initially. But I felt that perhaps he had talked about it so much that he had managed to get past the horror of the accident. It was much later that Mum told me she had instantly known Al was lying.

Mum eventually switched the conversation to talking about his job and he explained that as an auditor it was his job to review systems and controls and advise on improvements to company procedures, and talked through the processes and what he enjoyed about it. We chatted about other things including what to do the next day, and we decided upon a visit to the Sea Life Centre.

After dinner, Mum took a very tired Ben back to the B&B. Al was leaving for work early the next day, so they said their goodbyes. They were both polite towards one another and I didn't pick up any animosity between them or reservations from Mum's side. She hugged him and told him how nice it was to meet him properly and talk more to him, and she hoped it wouldn't be too long before she saw him again.

The next morning Mum and Ben came over to the flat for breakfast after Al had left for work and I dished up cereal and orange juice while we made our plans for the day.

'Are you looking forward to going to the Sea Life Centre?' I asked. 'They've got a giant, scary octopus and huge sharks that will try to gobble you up!' I pretended, leaning in to tickle Ben.

'Yay! Yay!' he squealed. 'Let's go to see the sharks!'

We walked the short distance into town, where we spent a few hours looking round everything at the Sea Life Centre while Ben excitedly pointed out all the different fish, sting-rays and turtles.

'Aunty Alison, LOOK!' he squealed as we rounded each corner.

It was late morning and Mum and I decided to stop at the cafe, which is right in the middle of the centre, with fish tanks on all sides. We sipped cups of tea, while Ben drank hot chocolate, the milky foam sitting on his top lip like a moustache.

As we chatted away, there was a tap on my shoulder. I spun round; it was Al, looking smart in his suit, shirt and tie.

'Hi everyone,' he said, innocently.

'Al, what are you doing here?' I asked. I had mentioned in the morning that we were thinking of taking Ben there but I was pretty surprised to see him.

'I left work,' he said. 'I had an external meeting so decided not to go back to the office. I thought I'd come and meet you – and catch up on some emails later.'

'Did you have a nice time, Ben?' he asked and the conversation moved on. I don't remember thinking it was odd, because occasionally he had worked half days. I thought that not coming from a big family himself, he was eager to get to know my family – and be a part of it. It's only later that I could see he was becoming possessive and didn't like me to be with other people. I don't think I noticed at the time, but looking back, Mum was very quiet that whole day, and even more so after Al's surprise visit. She admits that she couldn't quite put her finger on what made her feel so uneasy, but she knew that something just wasn't quite right.

One evening when we were in bed, at the end of July, I told Al I loved him for the first time. I felt happy telling him because I genuinely felt it. After I'd got used to him living in the flat, things had gone back to being really good between us and I felt happy and settled.

Al and I decided to go away together and have a holiday. My exhaustion was getting worse and worse as I worked my shifts in A&E, and we decided that a relatively cheap week in the sun was just the respite I needed. I was told when I would have time off – I wasn't able to choose – so when I knew that I had a whole week scheduled off, I suggested to Al that he book some days too because I wanted to make the most of my time away from work. I also felt I needed to spend some proper time with Al, because we hadn't had any prolonged quality time together since my placement had started. I didn't care where we went as long as it had sun and sand, but Al said he wanted to visit one of the Greek islands because he had heard they were particularly picturesque. He found a deal on the Internet for seven days on the Greek island of Skiathos, checked out the reviews, gave the holiday the thumbs up and I got on with booking it. I was keen to have something to look forward to and a week that might mark some sort of full stop in my busy working life.

It was when I was entering our passport details into the computer that I noticed Al's birthday was not in December 1974, like me, but December 1969, which meant he was forty years old, not thirty-five, as he had told me. I also unearthed his UK visa, which had said it was valid from July 2009, which indicated that he had been in the country for just a year, rather than five years. In some ways the revelation about the time he had been in the country made me feel better, and explained why he didn't know that many people or the UK and Europe that well. It made much more sense and helped a few things click into place. However, I didn't understand why he would lie about something like that, or about his age.

I mentioned it immediately and he was quite apologetic, saying he had initially wanted to make a good impression and felt that if I thought he was the same age and had been here for longer, I would be more inclined to consider him as boyfriend material. He explained that before we met and he had spoken to the agency, he thought it would look better and he would meet someone who was young at heart, like him. They were two small lies but in my eyes they weren't big game-changers – I know lots of people lie about their age for various reasons – and the fact that he had been over in the UK for less time seemed more of a white lie than anything sinister.

'I wanted to meet someone like you, Alison, someone who would give me a chance. I didn't want to meet a forty year old,' he explained. 'And besides, I still feel like I'm thirty!'

He had told me fairly early on in our relationship that he hoped to have a family at some point in the future, and a house with kids running around the garden, while he read his paper in the sun, so I guess that was part of his reasoning too. I knew he hadn't had much experience with babies or children because at my mum's wedding my nephew Aiden was still small and Al had been very excited to pick him up, all fingers, thumbs and smiles, as he negotiated not dropping him. I guessed he hoped for the sort of family life he hadn't had growing up, with both parents there and two or three children. So I just brushed the lies aside as nothing for me to be concerned about.

A week or so before the holiday, we were in the flat watching the TV and Al started chatting about jewellery and, specifically, rings.

'If you were going to have a ring, what would you like?' he asked, coyly.

My heart sank as I envisaged Al plotting some sort of romantic proposal. While I thought I loved him, I didn't feel anywhere near ready to be getting engaged. By then we had only been dating for six months and it felt way too soon. While I was happy to an extent in that moment, I still wasn't convinced he was 'The One' – the person I wanted to be with forever. I couldn't quite put my finger on why he wasn't or why I didn't know, but in my gut I knew it was too soon to be planning a wedding, and the thought of him bending down on one knee and popping the question left me cold.

However, I was aware that Al was properly into me – he told me he loved me all the time – and I think he was hoping to give the relationship a far more official footing.

'Al, why are you talking about rings? I'm not ready to get engaged if that's what you mean.'

'No, no,' he tittered nervously. 'I'm only talking hypothetically. If you were to have a ring, what sort of style would you like? I'm talking way in the future. I'm just intrigued. You girls and your jewellery; I never get it right!'

I immediately felt my shoulders drop an inch in relief. Every girl imagines their perfect engagement ring, don't they? *He must genuinely just be interested in the sort of styles I like*, I told myself, reassured that he meant nothing more by it.

'I love those rings with three diamonds. I saw a lady wearing one once and it had three stones on a gold band. It was beautiful. If and when I get engaged, I think I'll probably go for something like that.'

'What? You mean the ones with one big stone with two smaller stones either side?'

'No, three all the same size; I think they are lovely,' I explained. 'Whoever I marry won't be able to propose on the cheap! But I'm not ready for marriage yet, so don't get any ideas. Al, I'm being serious. Please listen to me,' I pleaded, not wanting to hurt his feelings but desperate to get my message across. 'Marriage is still a long way off for me.'

I laughed awkwardly, hoping I had diffused the situation,

and I switched my attention back to the programme we had been watching. A few minutes later when I looked over at Al, he seemed distracted and deep in thought; his dark brows knotted as he stared at the TV.

Skiathos is a beautiful and compact island at just seven by three-and-a-half miles and is almost unrealistically pretty, with thick forests, vast beaches and Caribbean-blue seas. We stayed in a small, red-roofed traditional Greek hotel, where the staff welcomed us with open arms like we were long-lost family.

The island had exactly what we were after, with loads of secluded sandy beaches, delicious seafood and a low-key charm. I would have been quite happy to do nothing and just relax on my sun lounger to completely reset and recharge, but Al was all up for exploring, so we compromised and on our first full day we walked into town and booked ourselves on to a couple of tours with a local operator: one island-hopping to the local island spots of Skopelos and Alonissos for the next day, and another boat tour for our penultimate day on the island.

The holiday was just what I needed after my A&E madness. We got up late every day and ate a simple breakfast of toast and coffee on our balcony in the late morning sun, admiring the delightful views. We then strolled down to one of the pretty beaches where we handed over a few euros to a man in an oversized straw hat to hire a sun lounger. We would spend the days lying back and watching families nearby chasing each other in and out of the surf or trying to make a dent in the stash of books we had brought with us. Sometimes in the late afternoon we pottered into the town centre, dipping in and out of the small shops selling local handmade crafts and postcards. The first couple of days we couldn't get over the large amounts of tours that seemed to be taking place around us. Gaggles of people swarmed past listening to their guide and we found out they had recently filmed *Mamma Mia!* there so the island was brimming with die-hard ABBA fans, humming along to 'Waterloo' and 'Dancing Queen'.

The hotel was self-catering and there was a little hob and fridge in our room, but we mostly ate out in the evenings, tucking into mouth-watering fish in one of the small tavernas dotted around the town, and afterwards we would often head to one of the local bars or back to the one at our hotel, which was quite lively. Skiathos was visually stunning at night; everywhere we looked there were pretty lights illuminating the town and it was hard not to be sucked into the romance of the place.

On our penultimate day we went off on our boat tour, sailing around the island. A couple of hours in, we docked near the beach of Lalaria, which is only accessible by boat and famous for its round, white pebbles, which look like shimmering marbles. It was picture perfect, like the scene of a postcard, and everywhere I looked were different shades of blue and pearly white. The tour organizer told us we would be there for an hour and we could go off snorkelling, explore the beach or just relax. The sea was perfectly calm, like a millpond, and I went off snorkelling for a while, following shoals of teeny tiny fish and admiring the pretty corals. When I waded back to the shore, flippers, mask and snorkel in hand, I could see that Al was grinning from ear to ear. I plonked myself down next to him, squeezing the salty water from my hair and rubbing it out of my eyes.

'What do you think of my sandcastle?' he asked, pointing out the structure he had made in the sand. The sun was so bright it took a while for my eyes to adjust, but there in the sand a few foot away from us was a pretty basic structure, made without the help of a bucket and spade.

I don't know why I did this but jokingly I stood up and kicked it over. That's when I saw the small black box peeking out at me. For a second I just didn't think and quickly pulled the box out and flipped the lid open.

Inside was exactly the ring I had described to Al, glinting back at me.

My stomach did a painful somersault as I tried to think of the right thing to say. My first emotion was annoyance because I felt this would leave what had been a wonderful holiday on a bit of a sour note. But I also felt horribly tense because I had told him that I didn't want this. There was no way I could accept.

For a few seconds time seemed to slow down.

'Alison, will you marry me?' he asked, his eyes sparkling and full of hope.

'Al, I told you not to do this,' I said quietly, unable to meet his eye, willing myself not to get too emotional.

'I thought you'd be happy,' he urged. 'I thought this was what you wanted.'

'I'm not happy. I told you that I didn't want this. I don't want this. Not yet anyway.'

'But Alison, I love you. I love everything about you. I want to spend the rest of my life with you.' Al seemed confused, as if we'd never had the conversation back at the flat. As if I had been talking excitedly about the prospect of getting married to him, not saying that I felt it was too soon to even consider it.

'Al, I love you too,' I told him. 'But I can't do this. Not yet. I can't accept the ring.'

'Then when? What are we waiting for? We're not getting any younger, Alison. It would be great to start a family soon, wouldn't it? And we need to get married first. You've said before that you don't want to be a pregnant bride.'

His arms were tightly crossed and the glow in his eye had turned angry. I had talked about having a family but at some point in the distant future.

'I don't feel ready, Al,' I said, welling up. 'I'm not ready and I told you that back in Brighton.'

'When will you be ready? Soon? Next month? Next year?'

I simply didn't have an answer for him.

'Listen Al,' I replied. 'I'll ask you to marry me as and when I'm ready to take that step.'

Looking back, I think I said this to make him feel better about the situation, but I still didn't know whether I did want to marry him. By saying this, though, it put me back in control. I hadn't wanted to think about life going forwards. With work and everything else, I was just coasting along trying to have the best time I could.

'Please put the ring on,' he pleaded, as I fumbled with the box, trying to give it back to him.

Eventually, I gingerly eased the band over my sandy knuckles onto my fourth finger on my left hand; my hands were a bit shaky but it fitted perfectly. He must have got my ring size somehow. It looked stunning and glinted in the light, but it didn't feel right. It could've been the ugliest ring in the world and it still wouldn't matter because I didn't want to wear it.

This wasn't how I imagined my fairy-tale proposal.

'It beautiful, Alison,' he said animatedly. 'It looks great on you. Please will you wear it?'

'No, I can't.' I was holding firm. 'You know I can't. I haven't accepted.'

'Please?'

'No, it won't feel right.'

Al seemed extremely agitated. I know he was disappointed by my reaction but I don't really know what he expected. Did he really think I would be swept up in the moment, momentarily blinded by the beauty of the surroundings and the ring and just say yes?

I took it off my finger and placed it back in the box.

Al grabbed the box back, let out a deep and theatrical sign and put it in the pocket of his swimming shorts.

'Please can we just carry on as normal?' I asked. 'You know I love you. I just want us to have a nice holiday and enjoy ourselves until we go home. Please can this not ruin everything? We've had a great holiday, haven't we?'

Al was silent and had turned his back on me.

*

Back at the hotel, we got ready for dinner, showering the salt and suncream from our bodies and hair and putting on some clean clothes. As I put on a touch of make-up, Al asked me to wear the ring again and I refused. I knew this was going to become a sore point between us for weeks.

Eventually I took the ring off him and put it carefully in my purse, telling him I would look after it until the time came that I felt ready to propose. When he brought it up yet again over dinner, to placate him I told him I'd wear it on a necklace when we got home. I just couldn't face the rows, sulks and silences, which I was starting to see more and more in Al if he didn't get his own way. If something triggered him off, he would become petulant and pig-headed, and I often ended up going along with what he wanted for an easy life.

I was determined to not let the ring incident ruin the holiday and tried to shove any awkward or anxious feelings to the back of my mind, but in my heart of hearts, I knew from then onwards that Al wasn't going to let the idea of marriage drop and the holiday had gone from being a fun, sun-filled week away, to something completely different.

He was now waiting for me to propose to him.

Five

The Inquest

The uneasy feeling Mum had had about Al from the day he turned up unannounced at the aquarium in Brighton hadn't waned. I was completely oblivious at the time to what was going on behind the scenes, but it was during one of my mum's regular Skype calls with Dave in Australia that she asked his opinion of Al and explained to him about what my gran had said. Dave said he wasn't too suspicious but he loves a bit of drama and gossip, so he suggested he would have a look around online to see if he could find out more about Al and his past via Facebook or one of the other social media sites.

Dave found nothing on the social networking sites but during his search, he unearthed Al's own website 'Legacy and Memoirs', which he had created using a Google domain name. In the opening paragraph, it reads:

In 'The Memoirs of Al Dhalla (His Legacy and Contributions to Society)', we discover that Al was an accomplished athlete, scholar

and gentleman. Al was a former military soldier and financier. His achievements have been documented into six categories: charitable achievements, academic achievements, athletic achievements, military achievements, family achievements and miscellaneous achievements. He had been a FreeMason [sic], Blue Lodge and Scottish Rite, for over 16 years and was a Mensa member.

Now I know what worried them most was that he claimed to be an orphan, yet there was still mention of his 'biological parents'. He also claimed that he was the first Canadian Ismaili, a branch of the Shia sect, to accomplish many things, including pilot a fixed-wing aircraft, fly a helicopter, scuba-dive, become a member of the Canadian Boy Scouts, work on the Canadian Stock Exchange floor and skydive from an extremely high altitude. They felt that the proclamations that he was 'denied employment, promotions, opportunities, service as a customer and social relationships by certain individuals and organizations for reasons of racism, prejudice, religious and ethnic intolerance for decades', and that he 'experienced incidents of racial slurs, bullying, harassment, threats and physical assault(s) for reasons of racism by certain members of the ethnic majority for several years', made it appear to them like he had a big chip on his shoulder about his colour. It was hardly as if Canada wasn't a multicultural place. They felt that his claims about being the first Ismail Muslim to do certain things was a little far-fetched, and given the number of Ismaili Muslims in Canada they were probably untrue, and the fact that he placed so much emphasis on having achieved all these 'firsts' in spite of Western prejudice suggested he might be inclined to self-aggrandizing.

He had made a great deal of his achievement during his teens but had failed to mention the things he had done in his early adult life, between the ages of twenty until coming to the UK. One of the biggest things that concerned them was that he had uploaded pictures of me under the 'family achievements' category, along with his previous girlfriends, who had all been blonde Western girls. Among them was one of us together at my mum's wedding, me clutching a bouquet of flowers next to Al in his suit, and ones of me in my swimsuit on holiday, flushed from the sun and smiling into his camera.

Alarm bells began to ring because the website didn't seem representative of the Al they had met, and Dave suggested that they should hire a private investigator to look into Al's background and his life in Canada. They agreed that they wouldn't say anything to me about it and, if he proved to be OK, then I need never know about it and they could all stop worrying about the two of us being together.

Mum and David decided to contact a private investigator but had no idea how to go about it, thinking it was the stuff of detective TV shows. David was still working and Mum had retired in 2008, so she spent some time online scouring the Internet, reading articles and researching the topic as best she could, pulling together a list of questions she needed to ask potential candidates. She found out that most private investigators' success was often to do with the strength of their mysterious 'contacts'. Some of them only worked in the UK, while others had contacts in other countries.

She eventually unearthed a man who used the name of

Elliot, and she ascertained that she would never meet him face-to-face and all the communication between them would be by phone. Mum checked him out by asking him to comment on Al's website and was very impressed with his findings. When she asked whether she could trust him, he shot back asking how he knew he could trust her. He initially went away telling her he needed to run some checks, presumably on her, but came back within the hour, which they saw as a good sign. She eventually chose him for the job because he sounded the most competent on the phone and said he had contacts in Canada. Mum and David concluded that he was either a former senior policeman or someone on the other side of the law, but they felt he took a personal and keen interest in the story. They told Elliot everything they knew about Al and made an initial payment, and he promised to get in touch as soon as he had anything to report back to them.

In the first week of August, Mum and David came down to Brighton for the West Dean Chilli Fiesta and, like Mum and Ben before, they stayed at a local B&B. I have always loved food festivals, regularly going to the one in Ludlow in Shropshire with friends, which is held in the grounds of the atmospheric castle there. I wanted to see if this one matched up. It featured chilli growing and cooking demonstrations, and tastings galore, ranging from the mild to the blow-your-head-off varieties of chilli and all different colours, shapes and sizes. There was chilli ice cream, chilli beer, chilli chocolate and chilli sauces, salsas and jams. We had a great afternoon working our way round the stalls, tasting the dishes on offer. Al and Mum kept digging into the hotter varieties and, by the end of it, they had tears streaming down their faces and were blowing their noses constantly.

On the way home we stopped at a pub for dinner. I thought it would be good for Al and Mum and David to get to know each other better. I didn't notice that the atmosphere was anything but polite and friendly, and Mum and David did a good job of hiding their worries from me. The conversation often revolved around history and Al talked a lot about his knowledge of British historical events, sometimes clashing with David over various facts and figures.

After dinner, when I popped to the loo, I later discovered that Al had asked if he could put an 'important question' to Mum and David, saying he wished to ask for my hand in marriage, and wanted to know if they had any objections. I hadn't told anyone about the proposal in Skiathos, hoping that if I didn't think about it, the whole incident would just go away, but I know they felt that it was very rushed. Mum, once she had recovered from the shock and regained her composure, told Al that she wanted the best for me and if I was sure that he was the man for me and would make me happy, then Al would have their blessing but it would be my choice.

I came back to the table to find everyone sitting in silence.

'Let's go on somewhere and grab a quick drink, shall we, before we all head back?' I said, oblivious to the tension in the air and the unease that Mum and David must have been feeling at that moment.

The ring was still an issue between us. I never did bring myself to put it on a necklace and instead it sat on the mantelpiece in the flat. Al had brought it with him to show it off, telling them it cost him £4,500. He was clearly out to impress. Now I realize that seeking Mum and David's approval was an attempt to put more pressure on me to get married, to bring me round to the idea of buying a white dress and walking down the aisle quicker than I had envisaged.

After the holiday I moved on from A&E and back to the GP surgery. I had loved being at the sharp end of the hospital but was happy to go back to having more regular hours and a slightly less hectic schedule. As part of my day in the surgery, I worked in a nearby palliative care home, where terminally ill people went to spend their last days. It was a very clean and serene place; it was how you would want a hospital to be, with personalized care, homely rooms and plenty of one-to-one attention. My job there was mainly to prescribe medication, make referrals to nurses, social workers and priests, and ensure all the patients' complicated medical issues were covered.

I don't want to say too much about it out of respect to the family of the patient but I was involved in a drug error, and a terminally ill man, who probably only had a couple of weeks to live, died a few days afterwards. I was at work when I was called into the office, where a consultant told me this error had been picked up and that they would have to report the incident to the coroner, who is responsible for confirming the cause of death. There would be an investigation as to whether the drug error had contributed towards the patient's death, she explained, telling me that the family had been told and were understandably upset and wanted answers. While the drug that I had prescribed was given at an acceptable dose, it wasn't the dose he was admitted on. An inquest was going to be held to find out if I was responsible for his death.

As I let the words sink in, I began to feel almost paralysed by shock and sick to my core. I practically staggered out of her office, a million thoughts and questions slapping around in my mind like a washing machine on a rapid spin cycle, and I realized how completely unprepared I was for something like this. Yes, I had done all my medical training; I had sat in dusty lecture halls until my bum had gone numb; I had sat studying mind-numbing textbooks late into the night. I had watched, listened and learnt but no one at any stage along this well-trodden path had ever taught my fellow doctors or me how to deal with something like this.

Somehow, I made it through the rest of the day, robotically doing my job, almost like I was having some sort of out-of-body experience, and it was as I walked home that I let the reality of what the consultant had said sink in. I reached for my phone and my hands were shaking. Then the tears started and I couldn't stop: would my years of training be for nothing? Would I be struck off the official medical register? Would my name be blackened forever? The worst question by a mile was the one that went round and round in my mind, like a stuck CD: had I actually killed someone? Was I responsible for a man's death?

Trying to pull myself together and swallow the sobs,

I dialled home and Mum picked up. I explained what had happened. She was the reassuring voice I needed to hear. Mum has a degree in psychology and master's qualifications in both education and business management. She was practical and helpful, reassuring me that the situation probably wasn't nearly as awful as I thought it might be. I needed to find out more, she said, and speak to someone to see what I needed to do. It didn't cross my mind that anyone else might be at fault; at the time all I thought was that I had made a catastrophic mistake.

'But I prescribed him the drugs, it must have been my fault!' I cried. 'I am responsible.'

As I slowly started to think through what I needed to do, it became clear how complex the situation was. If something like this happens in a hospital then it's a much simpler process because a consultant, with years of experience under his belt and skin as thick as a rhino's, would lead the investigation and everyone involved would write down what happened so the events could be pieced together like a 1,000-piece jigsaw and conclusions could be drawn. The investigation would be carried out internally and everyone in the firing line would be covered under the hospital's insurance. All doctors take out insurance, although if you work in a hospital, the hospital itself covers most of its staff's insurance. However, if you are out in the community, like I was, you pay for it entirely by yourself. By a horrible twist of fate, I was still training and wasn't covered by any insurance except my own, so I would be responsible for liaising with my insurance company and their lawyers to fight my cause and clear my own name.

I knew I needed to do everything correctly in order to continue my training and stay afloat. I was like a single buoy floating around blindly in a sea of administrative paperwork and legalities, attempting to make sense of what I needed to do and what had happened. Suddenly I found myself trying to make time for important phone calls to the legal teams involved, in a bid to work out what was expected of me and what I needed to write down. I found everyone evasive; the barristers wouldn't tell me anything and while I had two very kind teams of people around me at work, even the most senior staff had little reassurance for me. No one could tell me what the outcome would be. I felt that no one could help me and it was definitely only my problem.

The legal team I had been referred to from my insurer was there to help me write the reports and I had the relevant medical notes in front of me, but when I sat down with a clear sheet of paper intending to write down what had happened, I found my mind completely fogged up with thoughts and worries, my words all jumbled up in one messy heap. I have never had a complete mind blank before then but I just couldn't write anything; I felt immobilized, like whatever I wrote would be wrong and nothing could ever make the situation right.

At the time I was still working in the GP's surgery and thankfully this was a little bit easier than my time in A&E. I had regular hours and it was a job I had done before, yet my confidence was shattered and even simple prescriptions, like antibiotics, had me checking myself over and over again. I felt like I had had a sharp, stinging slap around the face and couldn't escape the constant fear that I might never complete my training or have my own GP's office, with a sign reading 'Dr Alison Hewitt' hanging on the door.

Al tried his best to cheer me up. He was kind and understanding, and each day when I arrived home I would walk in to find he had lit candles, had something cooking on the stove and had put some music on to try and help me relax. He cooked every night to make sure I ate properly, putting a plate of pasta or some stir-fry in front of me. I would shove it in and not really taste it, but regardless, having Al there was a far more welcome homecoming than arriving to an empty, cold flat.

While he couldn't actually do anything practical to help, Al did try in his own way and when the weekends came round he planned long country walks or other trips to keep me occupied. We travelled into London a couple of times for dinner and on another occasion he bought us tickets to see the stage show *Wicked*. Part of his motivation must have been that he wanted a bit of me for himself when we were out together, because I almost ignored him during the week since I was so wrapped up in my own world, but it still helped me to switch off a little from what was happening at work.

My other main confidante during this time was Mum. Because she had written loads of reports for her work over the years, I asked her advice on some of the reports I was writing and it was a great help to have a second opinion.

One night when we had finished going through a report on the phone, she told me there was something she'd been meaning to talk to me about.

'Oh, what's that?' I asked, intrigued.

'Well . . . it might be nothing, but did you know that Al has a website?'

I had no idea. He'd never mentioned it before, and definitely not shown it to me. Lots of people have their own websites nowadays as a way to boost their profiles or careers, but I couldn't think of why Al would need one in his line of work. And surely he would have mentioned it if he did?

'Are you sure?' I asked. 'Why would he need a website for his work?'

'Well, that's the thing – it's not for his work. The whole thing's about himself. All the things he's achieved in his life. And he boasts about some pretty strange things,' she told me. 'Please will you read it and let me know what you think about it?'

That's odd, I thought, but I quickly decided it must just be another example of his enthusiasm for everything and his desire to share that excitement with everyone else.

'Mum, he's Canadian and maybe he wants to list the things he has done. I'm sure it's nothing to worry about. Al's fine. I'm fine.'

'Please will you promise me you'll look at it? There are pictures of you up there.'

A chill ran through me, but I reassured her and told her that yes, I would look at his website. But when it came to my list of priorities, this just wasn't one of them, so I found that weeks went by before I actually sat down at the computer for long enough to discover more about the man I was living with . . .

*

I was busy working all day, five days a week and it felt like every spare second I had in the evenings, I was consumed with the inquest and writing reports. I was physically tired after my stint in A&E, and now back at the GP's I felt emotionally exhausted, too. I just couldn't cope with it. Every night my head would hit the pillow and I would fall into a sleep full of vivid dreams. I struggled to rouse myself in the morning and it felt like a real effort to put one foot in front of another. Work had gone from being something exciting, interesting and challenging to a job that I found incredibly hard, and some days I wondered if I was up to it. I continued to triple-check everything that I did and questioned myself constantly: what if I had missed something? Did I hear them correctly? What if I should've prescribed a slightly different drug? My brain felt bruised with the effort of just getting through the day.

The fear of the inquest and what I might have done lingered like a heavy weight on my shoulders everywhere I went. I struggled to move or even think under its weight. I felt so paralysed by fear that even the simplest of tasks, like taking a shower or putting some clothes in the washing machine, seemed to require an immense effort. Yet it was these small things and the routine of my day that kept me going and stopped me from retreating to my bed and pulling the covers over my head. Sometimes I caught myself browsing the Internet, looking for examples of registrars who had been struck off because of critical mistakes early in their training – those who had failed to perform the correct checks or stumbled under the pressure of work. In quieter moments, I even found myself looking for the worst-case scenarios, where if I were to be considered 'grossly negligent', then I could face criminal proceedings, charged with manslaughter and sent to prison. I was terrified but would just keep reading, my palm sweaty against the mouse and my heart racing. No one could tell me what would happen to me, so this seemed like it could be a possibility. I realized I could be the next doctor to be locked up.

When I eventually found time, I did log on to my computer and had a look at Al's personal site. I quickly flicked through the various pages about his 'achievements', although I didn't examine everything he had written in detail; I simply didn't have the time or the inclination. When I saw the pictures he had posted of us together on holiday, smiling and sun-kissed, and ones of me grinning back at him as he snapped away, filed under 'miscellaneous achievements', I was mildly annoyed but the whole thing just seemed to completely pale into insignificance alongside everything else that was going on.

But one day I decided to question him about it.

'Al, why have you got a website boasting about your achievements and, more to the point, why are there pictures of me on there?' I asked.

'Oh, that. When I'm old and retired, I plan to write a book about my life, so I set it up a while ago to document what I've been doing to help me remember everything,' he replied. 'This sort of website is not unusual in Canada.'

'But why are there pictures on there?'

'I put everything I do up there. It's no big deal. It's hardly a main domain site, so people wouldn't just stumble across it. You'd only find the pictures if you were looking for them.'

'I want you to take them down,' I responded.

Eventually he agreed, and thinking the situation was resolved I put it out of my mind. Looking back, I really didn't give it the attention I should have done. I wish I had.

At the end of August, we went back home to Aston Abbotts so Mum could help me with my reports, and Al and I decided to go on a couple of outings while we were there. On the Saturday I showed Al around Bletchley Park, Winston Churchill's secret intelligence and decryption headquarters during the Second World War, and on the Sunday we went to Mentmore Golf & Country Club, where Mum is a member, so she and I could do a class and Al could use the gym. The reception staff insisted that, as Mum's guest, Al must stay with her at all times, and he belligerently raised his voice, telling them he was an 'expert' in the gym and didn't need my mum with him. In the end, the matter was resolved when Mum said she would talk to the staff in the gym and explain the situation, but Al had shown a side of himself I hadn't seen before, one that was rude and condescending. I could see that Mum felt upset, too, and it was obvious she was holding her tongue for my sake, but yet again I brushed the situation under the carpet.

He's just having a bad day, I told myself. *Everyone does now and again.* But that was most likely the day when an uncomfortable sensation began to settle deep inside me, and slowly built as the months went on. Unfortunately I wouldn't pay enough attention to the warning until it was too late . . .

In August the lease for my flat needed to be renewed. Al had asked me time and time again to put his name on the contract but instead I renewed it without him knowing, just in my name. Despite the doubts I had about our future, and the ones that were beginning to grow about Al himself, I was happy being with him on the whole and enjoyed spending time with him, so I tried to keep an open mind as far as what lay ahead. However, one thing was for sure: I wasn't ready to give up my independence. So even though he was paying half the rent and we now shared it, the flat had always been mine, so it would be my name that was on the dotted line. It was also around that time that Al casually mentioned that his contract was up with LV, so he was moving on, but wasn't worried about finding more work because of his impressive CV. He quickly found a new role at Royal and Sun Alliance based near London's Liverpool Street doing auditing for other RSA offices around the country. The money was good, he said, and he seemed to settle in very well.

I think he probably coasted along at work and the main focus in his life was us – namely, when we were going to get married. Al was insistent that he still wanted us to tie the knot, sooner rather than later. He declared his love for me all the time and was desperate for me to propose to him. Having rejected his proposal on holiday, I could tell he was feeling more insecure in the relationship, but I was so consumed by my work that I didn't have much time to think about it.

As the weeks wore on, I slowly realized that I needed to work out how I felt about Al once and for all, as it wasn't fair to either of us continuing in this limbo. I knew I had to do some real soul-searching and work out whether he was someone I could see myself with in the future. Could I picture us getting married one day? Did I want to have kids with him? I wasn't sure. But whenever I tried to imagine those things, I found myself shutting down emotionally. I didn't feel like I could talk to anyone about it, so it felt like a huge challenge, one I just wasn't ready to take on.

Looking back now, I know that that was because of the ongoing inquest and the effect it was having on me. I had begun to doubt everything I did and found myself in tears all the time for no apparent reason; my brain felt constantly steamed up and murky. However many reports I painstakingly completed, there were still more to write, or the existing ones would come back from the barristers needing to be completely rewritten or restructured. Often I put off doing any of this sort of writing until the weekends because I was so shattered in the evenings, but when I came to them, my mind was empty and the screen in front of me remained blank, as I blinked away more tears. I was panic-stricken about where my life was heading. I had invested so much time and money in qualifying to become a doctor, and it was the only thing I wanted to do. What would I do if it was all for nothing?

My family suggested that I think about taking time off, so I could get my head around it a bit more and have a holiday, but as far as I was concerned I couldn't step off the busy conveyor belt that I was on, doing my various placements. Firstly, it would look bad and like I couldn't cope with pressure and, secondly, I would still have to do the placements and would face the uphill struggle of getting back into it afterwards. This was what I had wanted for such a long time, so I drained every last bit of energy I had into my days at work, seeing patients, asking questions and writing prescriptions. I knew people in the places where I worked were talking about me in hushed tones and behind closed doors; I was the one who had to face an inquest because of the drug error. I felt I had a lot to prove to everyone and that I needed to face the repercussions of the error I had made and not run away from it.

Throughout all this time the proposal was clearly in the forefront of Al's mind. On a couple of occasions I caught the train to meet him after work. It was early autumn by then and the evenings were cool and crisp. Al would whisk me cheerfully towards scenic or iconic landmarks, like Westminster Bridge or the Tower of London, where he would stop me and comment on the incredible view of the city, or how romantic it was and really gaze at me lovingly, all doe-eyed and soppy, as the sun dipped behind the horizon. In hindsight, I can see that he was eagerly hoping for me to pop the question and was laying the groundwork for the perfect proposal, but my mind was so far away from that that the thought of asking him hadn't even registered. I was in no state of mind to even be considering it. We continued to go out to sumptuous restaurants that Al booked us into and out at the weekends on walks and trips, but all the while I couldn't get away from the fact that my working life had become a nightmare. I was aware that he was thinking about us getting married but I was almost immobilized by stress.

The impact of the inquest was also starting to show in my physical appearance. Every day after returning from work and eating some dinner I would go straight to bed, feeling shattered. I fell asleep quickly but struggled to rouse myself in the mornings. Even if I had had nine hours' sleep, when my alarm went off it felt as if I had only been lying there for ten minutes. I felt permanently exhausted and I had huge, black bags under my eyes. My skin was dry and flaky and my hair hung limply to my shoulders. I hardly ever looked in the mirror but when I did I barely recognized the person staring back at me.

I didn't realize it at the time but Al was becoming all consumed with weddings. In his free time, he was scouring the Internet for local wedding venues and pretty churches in the area and researching English wedding traditions. He'd become some sort of invisible bridezilla imagining the perfect day for us, with lace-trimmed, handcrafted invitations and a three-tier cake with white ribbons, which we would cut together with a silver-plated knife, the first job we would share as man and wife.

At the weekends he would drop into the conversation that there was a great church nearby, or ask me if I had ever thought about what sort of wedding dress I would like, or what sort of colour scheme I thought would suit different venues. My way of dealing with it was by shutting the conversation off, or by telling him I was just happy dating at that point. I thought if I didn't engage with the wedding talk, it would just go away.

From my later training in psychiatry I now understand more about the dynamics of unhealthy relationships but when people ask me if they think Al eroded my self-esteem, or put me down in an attempt to 'keep' me for himself, I can honestly say that there was nothing left to erode; some days I felt that I had hit rock bottom. I hated my life, my work and my perceived incompetence.

However, he was starting to wear me down with regard to weddings. The more he talked, the less I engaged. I didn't feel I was ready to end the relationship, and I know I was stringing him along and that was unfair, but I felt like I didn't have a choice.

I think I had some sort of breakdown. Although I was functioning in the sense that I was getting up, going to work, doing my job and coming home, I felt like I had reached some sort of limit, physically and emotionally. I was paranoid and withdrawn. I hoped that once I understood my situation a bit more clearly, it would pass. I was also relieved that the inquest was just a few months away in December; I have heard of cases where the people involved have had to wait years to be cleared and the enquiry stretched on indefinitely into the future. I knew that it was only after the inquest had taken place that I could deal with the Al situation and sit him down and talk to him properly about how I felt and how we could move forwards.

But still, I tried to sort out the jumble of emotions in my

head and started seeing a counsellor. It was Mum who originally suggested that talking to an impartial person might help me. The first guy I saw had a large Adam's apple and was stuffy and unhelpful. In his sessions I would find myself talking a lot, while he nodded, gulped loudly or scratched his thick beard, as if his mind was elsewhere or he was equally puzzled by what I was saying. I was so deeply confused by what I should do about Al and how I could cope with the inquest that even having these sessions didn't help untangle my complex work and personal life.

However hard I tried to push all thoughts of weddings to the back of my mind, they remained very much Al's complete focus. One weekend in early September he started talking about us having a November wedding. Normally ending the conversation as gently as I could so as not to hurt his feelings, this day I just snapped.

'How on earth could I attempt to celebrate one of the happiest days of my life with the inquest hanging over me?' I said, the anger and frustration clear on my face.

'What about the new year?' Al asked, looking hopeful. He seemed to be completely oblivious to my feelings on the matter. 'The inquest will be over then and we will have a bit more time to plan everything.'

'Look, we can talk about it then,' I said, taking a deep breath. 'After all this work stuff is over, I promise I'll talk to you about it properly.' The only way I could cope with it was by postponing making any sort of decision.

One Saturday afternoon, Al suggested we go to look at a

church to cheer me up. I was feeling depressed and lethargic, like I just wanted to go to bed for ten years and never come out again. He suggested that talking to the vicar might help me with regard to the way I was feeling generally about my life. He could offer guidance and support, he said.

I wondered out loud whether not being a regular church-goer locally would mean that it wasn't appropriate but Al reassured me; that was the vicar's job. *Perhaps he will offer some words of wisdom*, I thought, and by then I was willing to try anything to get my old self back, especially because I hadn't found the counselling much help. What on earth had happened to me? I needed something and maybe that something was God? I wasn't thinking that this trip was going to be about weddings, although I knew Al probably had that in the back of his mind. He had brought up going to visit churches a number of times before and I had refused. In the end I grudgingly agreed to go, more for the sake of not having an argument than really wanting to see the church or talk to the vicar.

We walked down the road to a church called St George's and looked around. It was an impressive yellow-brick building and although it wasn't several hundred years old it had simple, clean lines and a nice sense of symmetry about it. It was surprisingly light and spacious inside with displays of fresh flowers after what must have been a recent wedding.

After a brief look around, Al guided me towards the lobby area where we sat down with the vicar, who was a man with beaky features and a lilting voice.

'Can you talk us through the marriage process?' Al asked

eagerly. 'Then, if you have time, Alison would love to talk to you. She has a lot going on with her work at the moment.'

Of course I shouldn't have been surprised that Al's priority wasn't my mental state but when we were going to tie the knot. Strangely enough, though, I didn't feel angry, just vacant and numb. It was almost as if I wasn't there.

They chatted for a few minutes about wedding bands and the official procedures in the run-up to a wedding. I noticed the vicar glancing at me on several occasions with a concerned look on his face, obviously sensing my indifference, so he kept his explanation short and punchy, rattling out a list of dos, don'ts and what happens when he marries a couple, and told us to come back when we had decided when we wanted the marriage to take place.

He turned to me and asked if I would like to talk to him on my own about what had been troubling me at work. I felt lifeless, like a zombie, and just wanted to get the hell out of there, so I told him as politely as I could that I would return at a better time and on my own.

During this time when I had been gradually shutting down mentally, Al had taken to emailing my family with pictures of us together, telling them what we had been doing with our weekends and how I was. Dave and Mark kept telling me that they didn't want to know if I'd had a romantic evening or to see three snaps of me sitting by a rock. I put Al's enthusiasm for photography and the way he emailed the pictures down to 'Al being Al'; he was enthusiastic about everything and wanted to share his happiness with my family. He had taken pictures of us together every time we had gone anywhere since he first came to Brighton and went on the boat trip, and I had got used to him snapping away. In some ways I was relieved that he contacted the family to let them know I was fine, because it felt like one less thing for me to do. Most days, I didn't feel like talking to anyone, even my brothers.

Al must've mentioned the possibility of a November wedding in one of his emails because one day my phone rang and Mum was on the other end sounding very worked up.

'You can't do it, Alison!' she said in a firm voice. 'It's far too soon and you don't know him well enough!'

'Calm down, Mum. I've got absolutely no idea what you're talking about. What do you mean? I can't do what?'

'Get married to Al next month! It's far too soon, sweetheart, and there's something about him that really doesn't sit well with me. Please tell me you'll wait a while longer at least.'

I stood holding the phone, not really knowing what to say. Surely Al wouldn't discuss something so important with my family before I'd even said yes? But I no longer felt quite so sure I knew the answer to that question.

I told Mum not to worry, there had obviously been some sort of misunderstanding, and that I had absolutely no intention of getting married the following month, or the month after for that matter. As far as I was concerned I still wasn't engaged, so I wouldn't be getting married. I also told her I would sort the 'Al situation' out once and for all when the inquest had passed.

I knew things were beginning to spiral out of control, but I still didn't have it in me to tackle the issue head on. So

I chose not to confront him about what he had written to my family, and managed to convince myself, for the sake of my sanity, that it had been a big misunderstanding, that was all.

One day in late September, shortly after the conversation we had had about a possible New Year wedding and the visit to the church, Al emailed Mum, David and my brothers with a 'save the date', which read:

Miss Alison Diane Hewitt
And
Mr Al Dhalla
Request the pleasure of your company
At their marriage
At St. George's Church, Brighton
On Saturday 12th February 2011
At 2.00 o'clock
And afterwards at
The Grand Hotel

Mum immediately picked up the phone and called me. I was walking home from work when my phone rang.

'Hi Mum,' I said, stopping to answer her call.

I stood for a moment as I listened to what she had to tell me, and felt my legs go to jelly. I began to look all around me for somewhere I could sit, and spotted a low wall so went and sat down.

'Hang on, Mum . . . I don't understand . . . What does it say?'

I was stunned. I never imagined he'd go that far. I somehow managed to regain my composure and tried to reassure Mum, saying that it hadn't been agreed and nothing was booked. But I still couldn't quite get my head around what he'd done. Who in their right mind would even dream of doing something like that? In my mind I figured Al must've made some sort of mistake. No rational person would act like this. Then again, I knew I wasn't myself at the time . . . Maybe I had given him the wrong impression? My head was whirling with thoughts and emotions.

I knew I could no longer put off talking to Al about the whole situation, and especially this. I was just annoyed that we would end up having another argument as I felt like I had no energy.

I don't think my words to Mum on the phone did much to allay her fears but she said she would pass on the message to Dave and Mark not to book flights home. She was obviously becoming increasingly concerned about Al's behaviour, but I ended the call as quickly as possible. I really couldn't cope with talking about it on top of everything else. It was all becoming a bit too much and I was starting to feel like I just needed to escape.

Six

The Holiday

At the end of October, Mum and David were going out to their villa in Spain following the summer rental period. They always did this twice a year, in March and October, to make sure it was clean and tidy and to have a bit of a break in the sun. Mum bought the villa shortly after Dad died and let it out to family friends during the summer. It is south of Alicante, not far from a resort called Torrevieja, which is very popular with British tourists. The villa is situated in a smaller town called Playa Flamenca, literally translated as 'flamingo beach' because you can often see wild pink flamingos roaming in the salty lagoons nearby.

I was absolutely desperate for another holiday, so they invited Al and me to join them; there was plenty of space for all of us. We planned to go out for a few days before they flew in and then spend the remainder of the week together. At the time I thought it would be a really good idea for everyone to spend some time together after the weird email battles. I knew there was tension between Al and Mum, and I figured that some R&R together by the sea would be just the tonic. I put their animosity down to the fact they just didn't know each other properly. Mum needed to get to know Al and understand that he was just naturally enthusiastic about everything, and I hoped that Al would see that my mum only had everyone's best interests at heart and wasn't intentionally getting 'involved' in my life, which she had recently begun to suggest.

By then, my regular phone conversations with Mum had become less frequent. Al had told me that he thought she was interfering too much in my life, and that she was preventing me from being my own person and making my own decisions. I thought he said this because he wasn't as close to his family and just didn't understand our family dynamic. Besides, I figured, families are never simple, are they? But gradually I had begun to dread speaking to her because I knew that Al would grill me afterwards about what she had said or asked. But I was sure the tension between them was down to just a few sticky, teething issues that would resolve themselves once everyone was kicking back in the sunshine together.

What I didn't know then was that in an attempt to get to know more about Al's family, Mum had tried to get Al's aunt's address from him. Initially, she had asked Al for her details, saying that she wanted to write her a letter to introduce herself and send a photo of the family. Al refused and said that if she wrote the letter, she could give it to him and he would send it on to her. The fact that he didn't want any uncontrolled communication between Mum and his aunt worried them. Eventually, by email, Al told her that his aunt's name was Gulshan Esmail, that she was sixty-four years old and was still working, but he omitted her home address. In the meantime, Elliot, the private investigator, had made some initial enquiries in Canada and advised Mum and David that he did not think Al was an orphan but gave no more facts. He also told them that details from his passport would help with his enquiries considerably, so they hoped to get access to those details when we were all away together. The trip was already planned by then, so it seemed like the easiest way to get the details they needed. They did not want to involve me in trying to get the information in case their concerns were unfounded.

The villa is lovely. There are three bedrooms: one downstairs, where Al and I were staying on a sofa bed, and two upstairs, one in which Mum and David slept, and the spare one. Our bedroom was off the dining and kitchen area and there was also a downstairs bathroom. Mum and David had hired a car and we all went out to eat together most evenings but we did our separate things during the day. I was happy to stay local and show Al around the town, where there was a colourful street market once a week. Or we would stroll to one of the nearby beaches, or go swimming in the communal pool next to the villa. On a couple of occasions, we took the bus up into the picturesque local mountains, which are dotted with olive trees and lemon groves. Mum and David tended to stay in the grounds of the villa complex and read their novels or do sudoku puzzles.

Slowly the constant chatter in my mind and feeling of dread in my stomach began to recede. My shoulders felt less tense, the bags under my eyes were starting to fade from a dark grey to a pinkier hue and I wasn't thinking about the inquest so often, not turning it over in my mind every hour of every day, like I was when I was at home. I knew that being in Brighton had started to feel like one big reminder that my life wasn't quite going the way I had hoped, and being away felt good and gave me a bit of perspective. I started to see glimpses of the old me and, on a couple of occasions, I felt myself properly laughing from the pit of my belly for the first time in months.

One afternoon we went for a walk along the nearest sandy beach, as we did most days after lunch. It took a good thirty-five minutes to get there and we would walk up the coast and do a large loop back to the villa. When we returned that day, we went straight to our bedroom to put down our bits and pieces we had taken with us. As we stepped inside, Al must've sensed something was different in the room – I have no idea how. He immediately headed towards the bedside table on his side of the bed and started rooting through his belongings. All his documentation, like our tickets and his passport, were in his bag in a neat and orderly pile in plastic folders. He looked agitated.

'Someone has been through my bag!' Al said angrily, sifting through his belongings aggressively. 'This is not how I left my things.'

'Are you sure?' I asked.

'Yes. How dare they go through my things? My things are

private! Your mother has been invading my privacy. How dare she?'

It was a pretty strong accusation he was making and while I love and trust my mum and I always have done, I knew she had her suspicions about Al and his past, so I immediately realized that if someone had gone through his things then it would be her. There was no question in my mind that this was wrong.

I had to think on my feet because the last thing I wanted was the start of World War Three on holiday. I began to feel my face burn.

'Can we think about how to deal with this?' I reasoned. 'I can see you're angry. Perhaps it will be better if I talk to them to see if it's true?'

I looked over and Al was shaking with rage, his face puce and his eyes bulging, in an almost cartoon-like manner.

'How dare they? How dare your mother interfere like this?' He seemed almost demented with anger and was shaking his fists, like he was trying to stop himself lashing out.

'That's quite a serious thing to be saying, Al. How do you know exactly where you left everything? You might have moved things without thinking—'

'I know *exactly* where I left them!' he shouted, cutting me off.

'But why on earth would she want to go through your things? I doesn't make sense.'

'Yes it does. It makes perfect sense. She's trying to find out something that she can use to turn you against me!'

'Well, she's not going to find anything in your bag, is she?'

I said, wondering why on earth he was making such a fuss.

He turned his back to me and ran his hands over his head.

'Look, let's go for a walk,' I suggested. 'You need to try and calm down and I'll tackle this later. I promise.'

I had never seen Al so irate, so I took his hand and we went for a very long walk, back to the beach again. I was desperate to calm him down and I hoped that some exercise would dispel some of the adrenaline that was clearly going around his body. I also hoped it would give me a bit of time to work out what to do. I felt really caught in the middle.

As we walked Al ranted, 'Why was your mother going through my things? I have nothing to hide. How dare she? How dare she invade my privacy like this?'

By the time we got to the beach, I remember that he was still really angry. I tried to change the subject on to other things but each time I did Al flipped it back to how he was feeling and how it was an invasion of his privacy. I wasn't able to get through to him at all. He was shaking his fists in the air, ranting blindly about my Mum and David and what they had done. I had never seen him angry like that before and I was stunned. I don't get angry that often; if I felt as strongly about something as he clearly did about that, my default reaction would be to cry rather than shout and punch the air. I understood his point of view – he felt his privacy had been infringed upon – but it never really clicked in my mind at the time that he might be angry because he had something to hide, or that he had been 'found out' in some way.

I should've done something there and then and dealt with it as quickly as possible, but I put it off and told Al I would talk to my mum about it first thing the next day, when I could get her on her own. I felt really confused about the best way to approach it. I just didn't want to make a scene and naively thought everyone would calm down and Al would be able to discuss the issue more rationally.

In the meantime, we all went out for dinner together, a meal that had been planned earlier in the day. To say the atmosphere was strained would be an understatement; you could have cut the tension in the air with a knife. Al and Mum were diagonally opposite each other and Al defiantly glared at my mum with a feral stare while she spent the whole time scowling back. Nothing was said about the incident and Al was completely mute, apart from making the odd comment about 'privacy' and at one point referring to the plot of a Hollywood film where all the children leave their mother because she is 'so awful', presumably some reference to Dave moving to Australia and Mark living in Norway. David and I struggled to keep the conversation on an even keel, or going at all. It was horrible and I found myself taking multiple trips to the bathroom and lingering over washing my hands and admiring the bathroom decor just to avoid the terrible mood. In the end, I said, 'Right, I've had enough of this. I want to go home,' and we all shuffled out. It was clear everyone knew what was going on, yet nothing had been said.

Back at the villa, far from being calmer, Al seemed almost manic with rage. We went to bed as normal but he couldn't sleep and spent a fitful few hours tossing and turning beneath the light cotton sheet. He lay beside me muttering angrily, while I dozed in and out of sleep and dreams, sweating from the heat of Al's body next to me.

'I promise we'll deal with it first thing in the morning,' I whispered at one point, but it seemed this wasn't enough to pacify him. I still felt like I needed time to work out how I would deal with it and just kept wondering what the hell was going on.

In the end, at around 5 a.m. while it was still pitch black and silent outside, save for the sound of a few crickets, Al got up and started bashing the furniture around and making a racket. Again, this was a side of him I hadn't seen before, but rather than finding it scary, he reminded me of a toddler who couldn't get their own way or a small child with behavioural problems. At some points it was farcical, as he bashed a chair on the tiled floor or slammed the bathroom door on the way back to our bedroom in an attempt to show how displeased he was. I never felt scared or threatened by him, just a bit bemused and frustrated. He clearly wanted to make everyone know that he was upset and that he wasn't letting the issue drop.

At 6 a.m., after Al had been kicking things around for quite some time, I climbed out of bed, pulled on the nearest clothing and told him we were going out for a walk. I knew he must've disturbed Mum and David, but at least with Al out of the house they might be able to get some sleep. I was sure that if they confronted one another there and then, a huge shouting match would ensue.

Again the walk seemed futile, as Al was boiling over and saying more of the same sorts of things about my mum, his privacy and the unfairness of it all.

'That's it,' he said. 'I'm leaving. I'm not staying here with them a second longer.' We only had four days left of our holiday but it seemed that Al was determined to cut it short.

I told him if indeed they had gone through his things – and by then I was pretty sure they had – then we could stay in a hotel but I was adamant that I didn't want to go back home. I had looked forward to this break for weeks and I needed the relaxation and sunshine. I didn't want to be back in Brighton with the knowledge of the inquest hanging over me. I needed that time for me. I knew it was selfish but I just couldn't go back with him.

As we returned to the villa complex, Mum and David were sitting eating breakfast on the stone porch and Al started yelling, 'You've been through my things! Why the hell have you been through my belongings?'

Mum and David seemed quite calm and David put down his spoon and spoke first, 'Al, we know you're hiding something. What is it?' They had clearly rehearsed what they were going to say to him.

'What? So you did go through my things? See, Alison? See? I told you they did it!'

They admitted that they had and went into what I later found out was a cover story.

David had worked in the defence industry for most of his career and his job then was in sales and business development. He told Al that his security clearance for dealing with sensitive material was regularly reviewed and he had just had to complete the latest questionnaire to renew his clearance. This much of the story was true. He then went on to tell him that he had to answer questions about changes in his family circumstances including if his family had new partners, which wasn't quite true. He said that having completed the first part of the review process, he was called into a meeting with his security people and advised that Al was not all he seemed. They said he should tell me while they continued their investigations into Al and his history. This didn't make me suspicious – I knew that in his line of work it was normal because of the security issues. Mum and David hoped that this would make it look like the company was investigating Al, rather than them being the instigators of any investigation themselves, and that it would spare me the indignity of knowing that they had been looking into Al's past. They also thought that it would mean that Al's anger would be directed at David's work and company, rather than at them. However, this idea clearly didn't work.

'So you see all we wanted is to try and find out more about you,' David said. 'Investigations are still ongoing. My job is not at risk. This is all very normal, but I'm afraid Pam and I have our concerns that you are not all you seem.'

'Not all I seem?' Al spat back. 'How dare you? My life has nothing to do with you! You have no right to go through my belongings.'

Then Mum started talking.

'The backbone of being in a relationship with someone is openness and honesty, and we're concerned that you are not being honest with Alison. Her happiness is our priority.'

Al roared back, crimson-faced: 'You know nothing about me. How dare you invade my privacy like this?'

'No, as we told you, this is about my job,' David continued. 'I am being investigated for work.'

Al shouted that he was going to leave and stormed inside to pack his bags. David followed him quickly and purposefully.

I sat quietly with Mum, speechless. Mum told me more about the passport and that they had seen that he had lied about his age and how long he had been in the UK. These two things I knew, of course, but what I didn't know what the fact they had discovered that Gulshan was listed as his mother in the next-of-kin section, not his aunt as he had told everyone. Clearly his parents hadn't been killed in a car accident and he had lied.

'He's hiding something, Alison. We're sure of it,' she said.

It couldn't have been more than a couple of minutes later that I could hear Al inside shouting, 'Your wife is a fucking bitch!'

'I will not tolerate that kind of offensive language in my house, now get out,' David hit back, assertively but calmly.

'You can fuck off too!' Al shouted.

The whole scene was slightly surreal, as if someone could press 'stop' on some sort of remote control and we'd all go back to swimming by the pool, or lazing in the sun.

Al appeared outside with his bag, hastily stuffed with clothes and belongings.

'Call me a taxi. Call me a taxi!' he roared.

'Where are you going?' I asked.

He ignored my question and continued telling me to call him a taxi, so I went inside the villa and called a local firm we had used before. I felt embarrassed by his behaviour and horribly stuck in the middle, but how could I go with him if I had no idea where he was going? Part of me thought he would head off for a couple of hours to the beach where he would rant and rave for a while and then he would cool down before coming back and sitting down with everyone for a sensible conversation about what had happened. He spent twenty minutes ignoring all of us, including me, standing rigid on the porch, and when the taxi driver turned up, he took one look at our faces and seemed to sum up the situation pretty quickly. Al got in the car, slammed the door without a second glance, and with a cloud of dust, he was gone.

We sat on the porch and talked more about what had happened and about Mum and David's discovery. I admitted that I knew he had lied about his age and how long he had been the country, but revealed that I didn't know that Gulshan was his mother, not his aunt. I didn't think there would be a sinister reason for this but felt an overwhelming curiosity as to why he would lie about something so basic and fundamental. Mum and David were convinced that his extreme reaction showed that he was hiding something and that he could be dangerous. I needed to know more about this man, they insisted.

They then revealed that they had hired a private investigator and that the information about David's work investigating Al was just a cover story.

'You did what?' I exclaimed. 'Why on earth would you do something like that?'

They explained how uneasy they had been feeling about

Al, especially after they had discovered his website and its strange contents, and how they had found it odd that Al was so open about some elements of his past but cagey about everything else. They also mentioned what my gran had said to them after the wedding. They were worried that there was more to him than met the eye, and were evidently very concerned about me.

I didn't know what to think about it all. I was obviously shocked that so much had been said and done without me knowing, and I was mildly annoyed, but I knew their intentions were genuine. And they seemed to have a point: the level of anger he had shown meant that he must be hiding something.

While we were talking, Al texted me telling me he was sitting at the airport and was getting a flight back to the UK and he asked me to go with him. I replied telling him I was happy to meet in a hotel somewhere, and would happily book us something, but I didn't want to go home. That wasn't an option for me. He refused and insisted that he was flying straight home to our flat. While I felt that he had just cause to be angry, I didn't understand why he would fly off the handle in such a massive way. What was he hiding?

I spent the remainder of my time away hovering around at the villa, making futile attempts to relax and read some of the books I had brought with me. Maybe I should've gone back home and finished the relationship with Al there and then after the way he had spoken to my mum. He had been rude and out of order, no doubt about that, but she had gone through his personal belongings.

His web of lies was starting to unravel and I was confused and angry, but also curious: *why would you lie about someone being your mother? Why claim your parents had died? What was that all about? Who was this man?* I thought I had the measure of him, but clearly I didn't and I wanted to know more. At the time, I didn't feel repulsed by his lies – I felt there must be a good explanation for them. But I was struggling to reconcile what I was learning about Al with the Al I knew, who was loving, kind and attentive.

Regardless of his feelings towards Mum and David, it seemed Al was still as determined as ever to marry me. On the day he got home, Al emailed Mark in Norway, asking him to be his best man at the wedding and he said he was happy to write his speech for him. He also attached a draft copy of his own speech, in which he thanked Mum and David for their support. Mark forwarded the email to Mum which she picked up on the last day of our holiday, telling her that he didn't want to be Al's best man, because he barely knew him. I refused to engage with this. I would sort it out, I told her, in my own time.

Mum and David also emailed Al, telling him that after his behaviour at the villa they no longer wanted any contact with him because they felt he told lies, he had failed to apologize for his behaviour and that they believed he was attempting to play family members off against each other.

I knew Al had been emailing Dave and Mark since he met them at Mum and David's wedding back in June, and I think in some ways he saw them as friends or some sort of extended family. With regard to Dave, I didn't see their contact online as such a big deal. Dave was always on social media and chatting to people; he's the kind of guy who always knows what is going on and who is dating who. I thought it was different with Mark, though, because he is much quieter and obviously has a busy family life, so has less time to talk, email or spend on Facebook, finding out what everyone was doing every second of the day. Paul and Al had never seen eye to eye and they seemed quite wary of each other. Paul didn't have a computer so didn't check his emails regularly and was therefore omitted from the email loop.

After discovering Al had been emailing them quite a lot, I had asked him a couple of times not to contact them but he had paid no attention. Then one evening after the incident with the wedding invite, I specifically remember telling him, 'This is the third time I am going to ask you, and the last time. I've told you twice before and you've ignored me. Don't email Dave or Mark.'

He looked quite embarrassed and sheepishly replied, 'OK.'

But I was starting to question whether he was really listening to anything I said at all. Gradually I was coming round to the idea that some of Al's behaviour, like sending the save-the-date email and the way he'd now acted on holiday, just wasn't normal. Before, I'd put most of his odd ways and strange behaviour down to the fact that he wasn't British, assuming we simply didn't understand each other properly because of our cultural differences.

Deep down, I think I had known for a while that the relationship was doomed, although I wasn't quite aware of it at the time, but during the last couple of days of the holiday I finally came to the realization that I didn't want to marry him. Obviously the way he'd been acting played a part in my decision, but that wasn't the driving force. I just came to the conclusion that he wasn't the man I wanted to spend the rest of my life with and grow old alongside. His wasn't the face that I wanted to walk down the aisle towards, and he wasn't the man I wanted to father my kids. This much I knew then.

At the same time, I didn't feel like I had the strength to break up with him. I knew arguments, huge emotional chaos and yet more tears would be on the cards when I finally got around to it, and, like everything else, I felt that I would be able to deal with it better after the court case. I know this probably wasn't fair on Al, but I'm sure I'm not alone in sitting in a relationship that I know isn't working out, or being in a romance I know won't last in the long-term. When Al didn't get what he wanted he was like a child that couldn't be reasoned with, and I knew I would need all my strength to end it with him.

I was also aware that my relationships with my family would probably need rebuilding. They were all starting to get a bit hacked off with the emails, the promise of a wedding that I hadn't agreed to and now this incredibly difficult holiday. But I figured I was close enough to them that it wouldn't matter if I waited a few more weeks to tackle the problem. *I will deal with it*, I told myself. *Just a little while longer.*

I would take the matter into my own hands and pull it into shape, just as soon as I had the courage, strength and energy.

*

When I got back to Brighton, Al seemed to have calmed down. He constantly made references to Mum and the fact he thought she was noisy and interfering and that she had ruined his holiday. He also started to say how she was racist and bigoted – two things which are clearly not true. It was evident that she was now public enemy number one in Al's eyes.

The day after my return, Al went away to Leeds for three weeks with his company to work in their office up north. He only returned at the weekends and I threw myself back into work, trying to put the events of the holiday behind me. I oscillated between feeling angry about the way Al had been and strangely intrigued about why he had lied about Gulshan.

The first weekend we had together, I knew I had to tackle everything that had happened and ask him more about his family, his past and the mysterious lies. As we sat down for breakfast, Al started talking first. I think he knew that I had found out about his lies and that there was no way we could ignore what had happened, so he wanted to tell me his reasoning on his terms.

'Right, I will tell you about my family and why I have lied about them,' he said. 'This is not something I want everyone to know and it isn't something I want to talk about again. I had planned to tell you in my own time but because of your mother and David, I am being forced to tell you now.'

He proceeded to explain about his family background and why he had created a fictitious past. His ethnic origin was Kenyan but hundreds of years earlier his ancestors had come from East India. He admitted that his mother, Gulshan, and his father, Zahir, 'who was darker', were of East Indian origin. He said that he had grown up through the years telling people Gulshan was his aunt ever since he was a little boy, and this had become a cover story to hide a less-than-desirable upbringing. His family was a nightmare; his mother and father had separated when Al was still very small. His father had since remarried and had another family but Al had no contact with him and had written him out of his personal history. He wanted nothing to do with this man who he labelled an 'asshole'. As a child, Al spent some time living with his maternal grandmother and uncle. I read between the lines that perhaps Gulshan and other family members colluded in the lie that Gulshan was his aunt because they were ashamed of the split due to their religious beliefs, and that they felt, because they were immigrants, that people were 'looking down on them'.

'It kept things simple and stopped people asking questions,' Al added.

He continued to tell me his story. He was brought up by his mother and grandmother, who he described as being quite 'spiteful', and as a child he led a somewhat solitary existence outside of school. He would just sit in a room in the house on his own and read books, which was why he had gained quite a lot of knowledge about different subject matters. He was very well versed in all sorts of areas and, whenever we had been with Mum and David, he would often claim to know more than them about a certain subject. I didn't put this down to vanity; I simply thought he knew a lot about a lot.

Al labelled many of his relatives as 'assholes'. He said he thought they were not good people and that they had no input in his life. He also claimed to be an orphan because he didn't want any interaction with these 'bad people'. He had a very black-and-white viewpoint of the situation. It was so far removed from anything I had known from my blissfully happy family that I was left quite dumbfounded, but I accepted his explanation.

I took the opportunity to quiz him about his CV. I had a version of it on my laptop for some reason and I had looked at it again since the trip back from Spain when he was away. I noted that while he had made a big deal of all his achievements, especially what he had done in his teens and more recently, there seemed to be a gap of a number of years in his twenties.

He then explained that he had been in trouble with the police a couple of times. When he went to university in Canada he was in the army cadets and he had picked up a belt by mistake and taken it home and had then been accused of stealing, he said. This seemed very trivial to me but he explained that they had taken it quite seriously and that he had been fined.

Then came a huge blow.

'There is something else . . . I have never told anyone else about this before. I'm telling you because I trust you and I know you will understand,' he continued.

My stomach did a little leap. *What on earth is he going to tell me?* I wondered, but I don't think anything had prepared me for what he was about to divulge.

Al said he had never had a good relationship with his uncle, and when he was twenty-three and had returned home from university having found a job in the city, his uncle came round one night and they had a serious argument and ended up in a fistfight. They were in the kitchen and after he was goaded Al retaliated and fought back with a knife. I think he felt proud of his actions, even though he must've known deep down that they were wrong. He said it was the first time he had had the courage to get even and that he had felt like he was finally man enough to deal with his uncle and stand up for himself. He didn't kill him, but his uncle had to go to hospital because of the injuries, which if they were caused by a knife must have been serious. Al had ended up in prison, although he didn't tell me how long for.

'I did my time, Alison,' he said. 'I paid the price. Since then I have gone back to university and studied for my MBA and have worked for different companies. I have moved on.' He then went on to describe all the jobs he'd had after having left prison and recited all the positives in his life.

I nodded quietly but as I replayed the conversation in my mind, and the words 'knife', 'prison' and 'hospital' reverberated around my head, I felt incredibly uncomfortable. To strike someone with a knife was a pretty awful thing for anyone to do, regardless of how much they had been tormented or whatever the history was. Al was violent, and this was something I had never imagined. However, I was so confused at the time that, alongside the feeling of disgust that was sitting in the pit of my stomach like a muddy puddle, I also had a tiny grain of sympathy. So Al had been to prison for fighting back after many years of abuse at the hands of a vicious uncle? Not everyone who goes to prison is bad and many people have horrendous background stories. I thought of my own impending inquest and reasoned that maybe I would end up behind bars. Therefore, who was I to judge these actions? At the same time his words made me shiver and freeze on the spot. Once again, I didn't know what to think.

Al admitted that he hoped coming to the UK would be a fresh start for him. He said he found that many people in Canada had a small-minded mentality and that he had been subject to many racist taunts growing up – and he hoped to escape his tumultuous past. He had originally hoped to go to America to pursue his dreams but it had proved easier to come over to the UK. He said he had changed his name a couple of times and used an alias, because he had disowned his father. 'Dhalla' was a name on his mother's side of the family.

After that conversation, I knew then that the relationship was definitely over. If I'd had any doubts at that point, the talk had really driven home what I already knew: that this really was the beginning of the end. I knew I could never be with someone who had intentionally hurt someone like this, whatever the reason. I realized that I didn't really know him at all.

Al stayed in Leeds and Manchester over the next couple of weeks, driving back to Brighton on Friday nights and then leaving again on Mondays. When he was back in the flat one evening at the beginning of November, I tried in my own way to tell him it was over.

'I don't think this is going anywhere,' I said nervously. 'I've been thinking long and hard about it, and I really feel we need a break. I think you should move out for a while and then we can think about it when the court case is over and my head is a bit clearer.'

'No!' he replied, looking at me with a steely glint in his eyes. 'We all make mistakes and I have now told you mine.' He seemed to soften a little. 'We have a perfectly good relationship otherwise. I love you. I want to be with you forever.'

'But Al, I'm not happy. I don't want to be in this relationship anymore.'

'Look, Alison, all relationships have their ups and downs. We're just going through a down. We'll be fine once the inquest is over. We can go away on holiday and everything will be much better.'

'But Al, you're not listening to me—'

'I am,' he insisted. 'I always listen to you. I love you. I love everything about you.'

Al became convinced that it was Mum's fault that I felt like this, and that she was the one who had come between us and pushed him away. I imagine he blamed her for finding out that Gulshan was his mother and unmasking the truth; she was a 'busybody', 'nosy', 'interfering' and her attention was unwelcome. It was Mum who had made me think that the relationship would not work, he said.

Sometimes Al seemed infatuated with me and would hang on my every word, discussing our future and bringing things into the conversation, like the fact I had once said that I liked the girls' names Lily and Rose so that was what we should call our daughters. But more often than not he was angry and would pick fights and raise his voice to me. He never listened to what I was saying and had an answer for everything.

Along with a growing sense of exasperation that he wouldn't accept it was over between us, I was starting to become embarrassed about the noise levels. We often heard our neighbours talking loudly or padding around going about their everyday lives, so I knew that they could probably hear us and would be wondering what on earth was going on. I could just imagine them rolling their eyes, with the words 'here we go again' each time Al piped up.

I was still so exhausted with the work situation. My stress and worry about what might happen at the inquest continued to roll round and round in my mind. I was so weary I felt like I could sleep for a year and it was still only the routine of my day that was making me function. The heavy burden that sat on my shoulders weighed me down. I simply couldn't cope with arguing with Al as well as everything else, so I left it and parked the issue to one side. I really didn't know how best to manage the situation. I couldn't move him out of my flat if he refused and I even considered moving out myself, but knew I couldn't afford two sets of rent. I hoped – and prayed – that once he got the message and I said enough times that the relationship was finished, he would eventually realize that you can't be a couple when only one person wants it to work.

Seven

Canada

Since Al had moved into my flat during April, everyone had warned me that I needed to know more about him: his family, where he was brought up, his schooling and his friends. What kind of life had he led in Canada?

I told no one about Al's damning past or his prison sentence now. I was ashamed that I had welcomed someone into my life that had done something like that and I knew that it wouldn't be too long before I would find it somewhere inside myself to finish the relationship for good.

Before we had gone to my mum's villa in Spain, we had booked flights to Canada. Al had been saying for some time that he wanted to introduce me to Gulshan, and show me around the suburb where he lived, on the outskirts of Toronto, and the main city itself.

Even after he told me about his prison sentence, I knew I would still go on the trip. I felt I had discovered the very worst about Al and that he wasn't an evil person, he had just had an awful past. I never once felt concerned that he would be violent towards me or hurt me; I felt safe with him and it was good to have someone to confide in as I headed towards the inquest. He was also someone I had spent almost a year with by that point, so I was inevitably interested in and curious about the things that mattered to him. Quite simply, while I didn't want to marry him, I did trust him, and even though by then I knew I didn't love him, I did feel fond of him still.

I also needed to go on the trip because, once again, I desperately wanted to escape my life in Brighton; I would rather be anywhere else and I thought this would be a holiday. By then the inquest was just a few weeks away and I was absolutely petrified. I felt that my life as I knew it could change in a drastic way afterwards and I relished the opportunity to get away. I thought it would allow me to catch my breath and give me some sort of distance from the stresses of my everyday life. I needed to get away and I hoped that spending some quality time together would allow me to talk more to him about the relationship and potentially breaking up and I hoped, naively, that this could be done amicably.

Flying out, Al was relaxed, calm and cheerful, and he was very excited and keen to show me around, planning various day trips and outings, like he had done in the early days when we had been together. We stayed in the house where his mum lived, on the edge of Toronto in an upmarket, residential area. It was spacious, comfortable and well furnished. He told me that after working for a while and earning some money, he had helped Gulshan buy the house and a car and he was proud of having managed to do that for her.

Gulshan seemed nice enough. She lived quite a simple life and took the train into work every day. She had a similar job to Al and worked in finance and auditing. She spent time with her friends at the weekend and had travelled quite a lot in her younger years, although because of painful arthritis in her knees she hadn't been out of Canada for a while. Al told her she should come to the UK, but she didn't seem too fussed by the idea. Appearance-wise, she was as Al had described. She was in her early sixties and a little overweight. Her skin was fairer than Al's to the point that she looked like she could be mixed race. She was very friendly towards me, welcomed me into her home and cooked us an authentic East Indian dish while chatting happily about her life. On two different occasions we ate out at restaurants with her and we made general conversation about our travel plans and the things we got up to at the weekends in Brighton. No reference was made to Al's troubled past or the difficult family history, and while it was clear she was happy that Al had met me, she didn't seem particularly interested in my childhood, work or family.

The relationship between Al and his mother seemed to be quite complicated. He had mentioned before that they had their differences. He said he had put a lot of time, energy and money into setting her up and felt that she didn't treat him with the respect he deserved; he claimed that on one occasion she had asked him to sign the house over to her completely, which he wouldn't. I wasn't too sure about his reasons, but chose to keep quiet as I didn't think it was my place to get involved. Whatever the true story, they seemed to get on well enough when we were all together and I didn't sense any bad feelings between them.

I started to feel like I was getting to learn about the 'real' Al. He proudly showed me the primary school he had attended and young children ran around the playground as we passed, kicking footballs and playing chase. He pointed out the ugly grey block of flats he had lived in as a child, which was in a far less salubrious setting. He showed me his friends' homes and his grandmother's home. I didn't ask any more about the incident with his uncle. Merely the thought of it left a bad taste in my mouth and I wanted to enjoy myself as much as I could. I kept telling myself I needed to make the most of the time I had left before the trial, and live every day to the fullest. As far as I was concerned, in a few weeks I could be struck off and having to think about a new career at best, or at worst would be hand-cuffed and sent to prison.

One day we took the bus into Toronto and were swept along the pavements with other tourists and city people dashing to their offices or out for lunch. That afternoon, we walked through the financial district, where Al pointed out the imposing and self-confident high-rise office blocks where he had previously worked. From there we headed downtown, where we sped up a glass-fronted elevator of the CN Tower, one of the world's tallest buildings. We ate at its restaurant, where we sat suspended like a balloon in mid-air as we admired the breath-taking views of the bustling city below.

We seemed to recapture the romance in a way. Al was affectionate and delighted I was there, and I began to experience some of the feelings I had had for Al in the early days again, if I didn't think too hard about the knowledge I now had about his past. It felt uncomplicated and exciting, exploring the city. He seemed to be back to the way he was at the start and was enthusiastic, upbeat and playful. The argumentative, antagonistic man-boy side of him had clearly failed to board the plane. We shared a room and slept in a double bed together, and I felt happy to carry on like things were fine for that brief time.

I also felt a huge sense of relief not to be being constantly informed by my family about what Al had done, and Al retaliating, telling me I needed distance from my mum and that my family relationships were unhealthy in some way. He completely stopped talking about weddings and about any plans he had in the pipeline regarding us getting married; he obviously felt far more secure.

One day, once we had seen the city, we took a coach trip around some of the more old-fashioned towns and villages, eventually arriving at Niagara Falls, where we spent a couple of hours admiring the awe-inspiring sight. In hindsight, as we stood there by this majestic spectacle watching the great muscular bands of water arch over the cliff face, I think Al was still expecting me to propose.

The five days went quickly and soon enough, we were back on the plane and I had to face reality again. While I'd felt closer to Al while we were away, I knew I still needed to end things with him as I could see no future for us. But even closer to the forefront of my mind was that in a matter of days I would discover my fate.

Mum and David were horrified when I left for Canada, and Mum said a number of times that she wasn't happy about me going, but I was determined to get away. Unbeknown to me, Elliott had strongly advised Mum to do all she could to prevent me from going to Canada because the intelligence he was getting from his Canadian contacts wasn't good at all. With me so far from home, in territory that Al knew well and with a mother who had colluded in the 'orphan' story, they later admitted they had visions of Al violently kidnapping me and forcing my hand in marriage.

To compound matters, it was while I was away in Canada that Elliot revealed everything he had found out about Al to Mum and David by a phone call one evening. He told them that he had discovered that Al had a violent criminal record, as recently as 2006, which involved the use of weapons. They were also told that he had served at least two prison sentences and used aliases. The Canadian authorities had imposed a ten-year Weapons Prohibition Order on him, which meant he was prohibited from possessing any firearm, crossbow, restricted weapon or ammunition. Furthermore, he had been refused entry to the USA.

They were horrified at the revelations, which proved that he was in the UK illegally because of his criminal record and that he was a threat to me. After careful consideration they decided that it would be less painful for me in the long run if Al could be detained and deported back to Canada. So they contacted the UK Border Agency, MI5 and the Canadian authorities in an attempt to prevent his re-entry to the UK. The Canadian security authorities reassured them that he would be checked and potentially prevented from leaving, but he walked back into the UK unchallenged. They were horrified and outraged both at the news Elliot had given them about Al's past and the fact that he could come back into the UK without a hitch. They subsequently went as far as making a formal complaint in writing to the Home Secretary, Theresa May, but never heard back from her.

When I arrived back, Mum called immediately and, when I told her I'd had a good time, she swore at me for the first time in her life, saying how 'bloody worried' she had been. I felt bad that I had caused her stress but with the impending court case just weeks away, I knew the break had done me good. As kindly as she could, she told me what Elliott had found out and I was deeply shocked. He had clearly committed further serious violent offences just a few years before and the news chilled me to my core. I didn't want to talk about it, though; I just could cope, so I ended the conversation as quickly as I could.

Back on home ground, I knew I had to face reality and was still trying to talk Al round to the idea that the relationship was over and that he needed to move out. After what Mum had told me, I knew I had to tackle it. Al still refused to listen, telling me constantly that we were just going through a rough patch and it would get better. He couldn't wait to get married, he told me; he loved me. He just went on and on and on. It was like he wasn't hearing a word I was saying and had made up his own version of how things were and how I was feeling.

I was struggling to cope with both his resistance and my ongoing troubles at work. One Friday I just couldn't face another weekend of one-way conversations and arguments. If he wouldn't leave the flat, I thought, I would. I told him I was going to a hotel for two nights to clear my head. I needed some time for myself to try and escape and think properly. Maybe I would come up with a different solution to the issue or a new way to handle him?

I drove myself to a Premier Inn in Arundel and checked into one of their rooms. Not long after I had arrived, I was lying on the bed, mindlessly flicking through the channels on the TV, and my phone started bleeping again and again. I just wanted some silence. I looked at the texts. 'Where are you?' 'Come home, we need to talk.' 'I love you. Please can we discuss this more?'

After an evening full of texts, phone calls and voicemails, and my phone buzzing so much it was as if it had a life of its own, I eventually turned my mobile phone off, only for the bedroom landline to ring a short while later. It was Al asking when I was coming home. I hadn't told him where I was so he must have rung around all the local Premier Inns to find me. I was so stressed I thought I would actually be better off in the flat if he wasn't going to leave me alone, so on the Saturday morning I checked out of my anonymous room. My head pounded and I felt a dull ache in my stomach. I had had enough. As I pulled up into the driveway, Al sprung from the door to come and help me inside. As soon as I saw him I knew that I couldn't tackle the break-up or handle him that day, so once again I told myself that I would put off trying to deal with it again until after the inquest.

I thought that once the inquest was over my energy would return and I would feel like the 'old' Alison, the one with a spring in her step and a thirst for adventure. At that time I felt like I was a hundred years old and as though I might just lie down and stop breathing. After the case was over, I would know what to do; my bewildered brain would be clearer and I'd feel stronger, I told myself. I could even move out of the flat myself, if Al refused to shift his things. I loved my flat but I was sure I could find somewhere else as nice. He'd soon come to terms with what was happening. I needed to live minute-to-minute, hour-to-hour, day-to-day. That was the best I could do right then.

While all this was going on, I barely saw or spoke to my friends. I had mentioned to my oldest and closest friends about the inquest but very few people knew that I was having problems with Al. If people asked me about him I was non-committal.

One person I did meet up with was my mum's neighbour Claire's son Nick, who I had been to school with. I think Mum had had a word with Claire, telling her that I was having a hard time at work and in my relationship, and he dropped me a line asking if I fancied going for a drink. By then, Nick was separated from his first wife and living near me in Worthing, a little way along the coast, and his girlfriend lived just around the corner from the flat. I emailed him back, telling him I'd love to see him again. When I arrived back from our drink, Al came straight to the door and didn't even let me take my shoes off before he began firing questions at me: what did he do? Did you like seeing him? What went wrong with his marriage? Why was he separated? Who was his girlfriend? It was bizarre, but by then I had noted that there were many things that weren't normal about Al.

Unsurprisingly, Mum and David were far from impressed with the situation. Unbeknown to me, the number of emails from Al to my mum had accelerated, with him sending seventy-odd pictures of us from our trip to Canada, despite David asking him not to contact them at all. It seems Al was also keeping a one-sided series of events documented, and he regularly informed Mark and Dave what was happening and how awful Mum was and how she was the catalyst in any problems between us all. At this point, with the inquest just days away, I think Mum tried to keep the worst emails from me. One day on the phone, she brought up the information that Elliot had revealed again, but I brushed off what she said. I knew the details of his past, I told her, and this was partially true. I knew he had had a difficult past and he had moved on. She complained that Al had been emailing my brothers trying to turn them against her. I just kept telling her that I would deal with Al as soon as the inquest was over. I couldn't cope with the arguments.

Mum wrote me one email which particularly hit home. She said that she thought I had lost my sparkle and that I was no longer, the free, independent thinker they knew.

She added:

You have become secretive and distanced. We hardly dare phone or contact you as we are made to feel we are intrusive. The Alison who we all know and love is strong, has a mind of her own and rejects all manner of unkindness and evil (especially when it harms other people). She has a strong sense of justice, is responsible, sensible and a mature young woman who loves and cares about her family, all of whom are extremely proud of her and her achievements. Her future prospects used to looked so good but now seem fairly bleak. Very sadly and with considerable pain I now have to say to you, Alison, that I no longer have any confidence in your ability to make wise decisions and use sound judgement. You appear disempowered and seem to have lost control of your life. Worse still, you have chosen to believe and defend the lies of others rather than listen to and accept the truth from your family.

Reading back that letter now is far more upsetting than it was then. At the time, I knew she was right but I felt unable to do anything. I felt completely numb.

Mum also told me that she guessed that Al was reading my emails. She could tell how controlling he was and said that it was obvious he knew all my passwords and was studying my correspondence before I had the chance to. There was now nothing in my life anymore that was completely private or entirely my own. To be fair, none of my passwords were particularly hard to work out; I did leave my computer and phone out all the time on the table or mantelpiece, when I was in the shower and so on, so I knew she was probably right. What he was looking for, I have absolutely no idea, because I had nothing to hide. But from time to time, I would even find him looking over my shoulder when I sent the odd text message or email. He asked questions about everything and our conversations had gone way past the point of being normal coupley chitchat.

On one occasion, after Nick and I had exchanged a few emails and texts and talked about going for another drink together, Al begged to look at the texts we had sent each other.

'I want to see them, Alison,' he pleaded. 'Please let me see them. I need to.'

'Why? He has a girlfriend. I'm not hiding anything from you.'

'Well, if you're not hiding anything, why won't you let me see them? *Why?*'

Despite the fact that Nick had a girlfriend, Al seemed convinced that our friendship was more than platonic and I was concealing something from him.

A day or so later, just to satisfy myself that Mum was right, I told him I was going to the loo and left my phone innocuously on the table. I exited the room but rather than going to the bathroom, I left it a few seconds and came back. Al had his back to me but, as I walked in, I could see he was looking at my phone, eagerly scrolling through my messages.

'What do you think you're doing?' I asked.

He quickly dropped the phone and spun round, looking flustered. 'Well . . . I only wanted to look at your messages from that Nick guy . . . I wanted to check he didn't have the wrong idea or anything . . .' He was trying to look sure of himself but his voice had trailed off.

'So what makes it OK for you to invade my privacy when you went so ballistic about Mum and David on holiday?'

'That's completely different!'

'I don't see how!'

The argument went on in much the same way, with nothing I said getting through to him. He had gone crazy when my parents invaded his privacy, yet here he was doing exactly the same thing to me. I was fed up of fighting but Al couldn't see that he was being unreasonable and possessive.

From then on I kept my phone close to me, sometimes even stashing it in my knickers. I had nothing to hide, but I needed something that was just mine.

I know now that at this time Mum was frantic with worry about me. I had all but switched off to her warnings about Al, but later she said she had been suffering from sleepless nights and tearful episodes herself with the stress of everything that had been happening. Just to add to everything that she was feeling about my relationship with Al, she was trying to spend as much time as she could with my grandpa, who had dementia, which appeared to be worsening.

About a year before she had persuaded him to go on a 'holiday' to a care home in the next village, Wing, just a few miles from Aston Abbotts. He was ninety-five by then and very frail, but much to everyone's relief he took very well to his new home, where he became known for his mischief and his singing. The care home staged a number of concerts and held regular church services, at which he sang with gusto – not always the right words or even the correct tune, but always with enthusiasm. Mum had visited him almost every day and, after her wedding, someone collected him and he was brought round to the house and had beamed with pride to have his entire family around him. However, at that time he was having recurrent chest infections and seemed weaker and frailer, and often he failed to recognize Mum when she visited. I had made a point of going to visit him too, and he was sat in bed, small and pale. Al had insisted on coming with me. I'd chatted to him and told him what I had been doing and about my placements and the different places I had been since I had last seen him. As I'd kissed him goodbye and walked away, I'd known it might be the last time I saw him.

During the final weekend of November, Mum and I decided to go to a spa in Basingstoke. As well as being keen to get me away from Al, she knew it was just two weeks away from the inquest and that we both needed a break – and some time together. I imagine that she thought that if she got me on my own, she might be able to get through to me. I think she genuinely thought that I hadn't tried my hardest to break up with Al and didn't appreciate that he just wouldn't move out, despite the different approaches I had tried. We went to the gym together, went swimming in the huge spa pool and enjoyed the evening meal, but mentally and emotionally I was still struggling with the combination of stress over the inquest and my futile attempts to finish my relationship. This relaxation time together was constructive, but I spent a lot of my time alone trying to suppress the tears that I felt might start and just not stop.

By then I had switched to a new counsellor, who had pointed out that I was bottling up a lot of my emotions and that I had stopped letting myself be vulnerable. She warned me that invariably when people repress their emotions, they still come out somewhere along the line, but I knew that if I let them out then, there would be a cascade of tears and I would lose it completely. If that happened then I wouldn't be able to function properly at work or in my everyday life, and for that reason I just had to do what I was doing.

One of the exercises that I remember doing with her was one where she laid out lots of pictures from different magazines on the floor. She asked me to pick up and talk about the images I felt some sort of connection with. The ones I chose were always dark and macabre. I remember a picture of a wet, black cat screeching, its claws stretched out to attack and its yellow eyes glaring evilly into the distance. Another was a picture of someone standing on the edge of a cliff, their hair wild in the wind and their face blurred out. I surprised myself with the pictures that I picked and how horrid they were. It seemed like I had done such a good job of masking my feelings, I had even managed to trick myself.

I hadn't told Al where I had gone to the spa and kept it vague, explaining that the hotel was an hour and a half away. I hoped he would get the message and move out while I was away. By then, I was treating him like some sort of annoying flatmate who lingered around the place. I didn't confide in him about work or my thoughts or worries, and I had stopped talking to him about the inquest. I am used to people acting rationally, even if they are upset or angry, but Al had turned into a sort of person I'd never had to deal with before. He just wasn't getting the message and seemed to have an excuse or reason for every eventuality. I kept telling myself that Al was a rational person, he wasn't deranged, and while he had a temper, he wasn't crazy. He would realize at some point that my heart and soul weren't in this and he would come round. Besides, who wants to be with someone who doesn't want to be with them? I am a strong and independent woman and I had a lot of support from my family, even if they were still angry with me, so I thought I could deal with the situation by myself. Unfortunately it would take me a while longer to realize that I was wrong: this wasn't something that I could cope with on my own.

After I arrived back from the spa, Al asked me how it had been; but more worryingly, he told me that he knew the room had been booked under my mum's name. I hadn't told him I was going away with her; instead I had said I was going with my friend Claire. I knew that if I told him he would start talking about how Mum was trying to get me away from him and how she hated him. However, Al had clearly been determined to find out where I was and had rung around all the spas in an attempt to locate me. This worried me. I started to realize that wherever I went he would be checking up on me. A chill ran down my spine. *Just when will he get the message?* I wondered. *I'm not sure how much more of this I can take . . .*

*

The situation and Al's behaviour was magnified when I started my placement in the psychiatry department at the start of December. My job involved working in addiction services so I was based in the outpatients department at the main hospital. I conducted general medicals on people who misused drugs and alcohol and I signed prescriptions for drugs like methadone for recovering heroin addicts. I also sat in on counselling groups, where people discussed their journeys and supported one another as they came off hard drugs and alcohol. There was one ward in the hospital which specialized in detoxification, where we did our best to support patients who lay on their beds, sweating and agitated, determined to see their detox through. When I was on call, I covered the psychiatric hospital for older patients which specialized in dementia, as well as the general psychiatric hospital nearby that also contained an A&E, so if someone turned up saying they felt suicidal, I would assess their needs and either admit them, or refer them on to the mental health team to be seen at a later date.

I was seeing some pretty desperate people day in, day out, who lived on the very edges of society, many of whom would never be mentally stable or lead ordinary lives with families and jobs. At first the change was enormous after working in the GP's surgery, but as I got into the job it was clear that as a doctor I was only involved in certain aspects of patient care, mainly focusing on assessment and medication. I couldn't get emotionally involved but just tried to utilize the training I had been given to determine who the critical patients were and how we could help them.

Many of the patients had excellent notes, having been in and out of the services for years, and it was very rare to see someone who was unknown to the system. The most extreme cases I was involved with were the ones I saw in the intensive care unit of the psychiatric hospital; it was here that many people came in handcuffed by police after being sectioned against their will. I was aware that I was in danger of being attacked, but I was surrounded by people who were specially trained in things like restraint and there were systems in place so we were never in danger.

As part of my work, I had to go round and conduct risk assessments. I would talk to patients about their past and look into whether they had a history of violence or self-harm, to see if they were at risk of hurting themselves or someone else. Often it was the nurses that did these assessments, but sometimes the doctors would too. If someone had a history of violence towards another person, they were immediately deemed at 'moderate' risk of harming someone again. If the history of violence was exacerbated by alcohol, then they were considered to be at less risk because obviously they didn't have access to alcohol in the hospital. When I started thinking about my own situation it was becoming painfully clear that things with Al were far from ideal; I was already officially at a 'moderate' risk of being harmed. I found it almost impossible to reconcile this with the man I knew. I could see he had a temper but I could never, ever imagine him physically hurting me.

When I was approaching a difficult patient or one who was known to be moderate or high risk, I automatically felt more on guard and informed other staff that I was going to see that person, or left the doors open so I could escape easily. With particularly high-risk patients, we would approach them in pairs. The irony wasn't lost on me that I was taking so much care in my work yet was returning home to someone who was potentially violent. I wondered how I would feel if Al was on my ward, rather than in my house. This man was in my home; he wasn't in a secure and controlled environment.

All of a sudden I realized that I had allowed myself to be placed in what was actually a very scary situation for far too long. Al wasn't just an annoying problem to be dealt with when I felt up to it; he was actually a threat and I was putting myself in danger on a daily basis . . .

The inquest was held in the second week of December 2010. I only spoke on the phone to the legal team, who were brought on board by my medical insurer to help me, a week before the inquest took place, even though I had written numerous reports for them and communicated at length with them beforehand by email. My solicitor, the head of the legal department there and I, had a three-way conversation and we talked properly through the case. They told me they had found me a good barrister but at no point did they discuss possible outcomes of the case. This made me feel terrible and, once again, I had images of myself in prison scrubs. One time, I remember saying, 'I'm worried about a manslaughter charge,' and they asked me who had mentioned it. When I said no one, and that it was just what I thought would be a worst-case scenario, they didn't respond. One of them swiftly changed the subject and that was that. As far as I was concerned, anything could happen to me.

The evening before the big day, I met the barrister and solicitor in the local Travelodge bar where they were staying to talk about what had happened to get the barrister up to speed. The female solicitor was fresh-faced, young and enthusiastic. I decided that she must have only recently qualified, while the barrister was much older, greyer and clearly experienced in his field. He spoke with a reassuring air of conviction and had an owlish look about him.

We ran through all the reports again and they prepped me as best they could for the following day. The barrister told me to speak clearly, to answer the questions succinctly and to always keep an eye on him for direction. I felt sick with nerves and could barely even swallow sips of the drink I had ordered. My skin prickled with fear about what lay ahead.

It was hard to know who I wanted to have in the actual courtroom to support me. Of course Mum and David insisted on coming down, as did Al, and I was worried about how they would be with each other. But I had to put my fears to one side; my life and career were on the line. When they all arrived, Al sat in the back row on one side of the courtroom and Mum and David sat nearer the front to another side, and they ignored each other as if they had never met. Just before the proceedings started and the judge took her seat, Mum came and squeezed my hand and wished me luck.

The court used the patient's notes to follow his whole journey, from the hospital and the wards he had been in, through to the hospice. Of course, I had to stand up and talk about what had happened and give my version of events. The man's wife, children and family were all there sitting near the front, staring back at me and asking questions throughout the event, in glassy, emotional voices.

As the morning wore on, it was clear everyone was keen for it to be over with, so the conclusions could be reached and everyone involved could move forwards with their lives. The thirty to forty doctors, nurses, consultants and managers involved could go back to their work and the family could grieve properly for their loved one knowing the truth about his death. I had no idea so many people would be implicated – in my mind it had been just me who was potentially liable.

After a break for lunch, the conclusions were drawn. Drug errors do happen from time to time, of course – mistakes are a part of human nature. But I was starting to see that when there are errors in someone's medical care, there would be multiple errors and it wasn't just me who was at fault. When the coroner summarized the proceedings and delivered her verdict, she said that there was a 'failing in systems' and there were bigger factors at large. I was told that I was exonerated and there would be no repercussions for me. She said that I had been badly let down by the system, which failed to give me the information, advice and support that the normal procedures should have provided. Other individuals involved did not come off so lightly, but I had never even considered that this might be the case. I was amazed because I had prepared myself for the worst.

I don't think I'd really understood what the coroner's court was beforehand. The court itself is responsible for investigating the cause of death when it is unknown, but I wasn't personally on trial, which I had previously believed myself to be. I thought I would end up in a criminal court or, at the very least, be struck off by the General Medical Council. I thought it would be exactly the same as standing trial in a criminal courtroom.

Since my inquest, of course, many of my colleagues have now been involved in inquests, which are a normal and important part of investigating various deaths. However, being the first of my peer group to stand up and be grilled about something was terrifying and soul-destroying. My fears and terror had been completely unfounded; my mistake was just one part of a huge puzzle that I had been unaware of.

My first reaction was immense relief, like a huge iron weight had been lifted from my shoulders and ribs and I could actually breathe again.

'You can speak to the family now, if you wish,' my barrister told me.

Shakily, I stood up and made my way over to the family, who were standing on the other side of the room, speaking in hushed tones with a resigned air of relief on their faces too. I apologized to the man's wife for the fact that they had had to go through the case and acknowledged how hard it must've been for them. She graciously said the same back to me and wished me luck in my training. I felt like I had made my peace with them and, for me, it was the best conclusion I could've hoped for.

Al slipped out before I spoke to Mum and David, who told

me that they had to go back to Aston Abbotts because Grandpa wasn't well. Grandpa had actually died that morning but Mum kept the news from me until the next day – and while I was very sad, I wasn't shocked and I was relieved that his passing had been peaceful. In the end, I went to a pub with one of the other doctors who had given evidence, where we ordered large glasses of wine, gulped them down quickly before ordering another, and talked over the events of the day. The doctor I was with had a few more years under his belt and admitted that, while they knew it was serious, he'd doubted that any one person would have the finger pointed at them.

Walking back home felt almost surreal. The iron-heavy weight had been lifted from my shoulders and I felt freer than I had done in a long time. The inquest had dominated so much of my waking thoughts that the fact it was now over made me feel calmer and my head seem clearer. That night I fell into the first deep, dreamless sleep I'd had in a long while.

Back at work, I felt lighter as I walked through the various wards. I still questioned everything I did, but I no longer felt like I was guaranteed to fail in some way and I could finally carry my head high once again. I felt able to discuss what had happened, and my colleagues were eager to know more about what was said and how the whole thing had played out. My suspicions about the case being talked about and debated behind my back while the investigations were taking place had proved correct, but now I had been cleared I guess people felt they could ask me about it. I answered their questions honestly and briefly but I never really admitted to anyone apart from those closest to me about how I had conjured up the worst possible outcome in my head. I didn't want anyone else to know that I had allowed myself to go to such a dark place. I finally had the strength to attempt to rebuild my life – that was all that mattered.

With the inquest behind me I knew I now needed to turn my attention to my relationship with Al, so I started thinking about a different strategy to handle the break-up because the conversations clearly hadn't worked. I knew I still needed to figure out a way to get Al to accept that the relationship was over and move out. However, although I felt much happier and stronger than I had in a long time, I was still far from my old self, and I just needed to have a brief respite from drama and stress. I needed to allow myself to breathe and recuperate. By then, I was a bit resigned to Al being there against my wishes and the weekend before Christmas, desperate to have some normality and even some sort of fun in my life, we even went into London together and visited Hyde Park's Winter Wonderland, where we drank mulled wine and admired the festive surroundings.

But by Christmas Eve I was at my wits' end. The arrival of the holiday season had highlighted in my brain just how stubborn Al was being because he must have known that I didn't want to spend my precious few days off with him. I decided that I would try to tell him one last time that it was over. Finished. End of. No more. I wouldn't take no for an answer; I'd be strong and hold firm. Finally, I felt the strength to do this. I resolved that rather than staying in the flat, which is what I had done before, I would go out with him. At home, Al would argue back and we would end up rowing. It would always end when I just couldn't cope with him anymore and I would either go to bed and crash out, or head out for a walk on my own, thus removing myself from the situation. I also continued to feel embarrassed about Al's loud and shouty voice. Goodness knows what the neighbours thought was going on.

Around us houses were lit up with twinkling Christmas lights and trees glowed out from people's living rooms, hanging with gold, silver and red decorations. I could see families in their front rooms, gathered around the TV, and somewhere in the distance I could hear a faint rendition of 'I Wish It Could Be Christmas Everyday'. It brought home just how much I didn't want to be with Al because it's the one time of year that you should be with the people you love the most and, by now, I was feeling increasingly indifferent towards him. It really pressed home how awful the latter part of the year had been in lots of different ways.

As we walked around the block, I was as forceful as I could be and my message was clear. I had rehearsed what I was going to say in my mind numerous times and I refused to let him interrupt me or try to find a counter argument.

'Al, we have to talk. You've got to listen to me this time. The relationship is over,' I said, without looking at him, striding purposefully ahead. 'I need you to move out and start looking for somewhere else to live. You need to stop contacting my family and talking about weddings. There will be no wedding. I do not want to marry you. The relationship is over.'

Unsurprisingly, Al came back with his age-old pleas.

'But Alison, we get on so well,' he said. 'I love you. I've been upfront and honest with you and told you everything there is to know about me. I know we can get over this.'

I was quick to respond. I wasn't going to let him quieten me into submission this time. 'It's not about that, Al. This is about our relationship and it's over—'

'This is exactly why I don't tell people about my past because once they know the truth, they make a judgement,' he ranted. 'See why I had to lie? It's not so wrong lying about your past, is it, when people always turn their back on you once they know the truth?'

'It's not that, Al. It's not about your past. This is about us and now and it's just not working.'

He continued, 'We can make it work! You can't run as soon as the going gets tough. Relationships have ups and downs and this is our down. We can make it work.'

Feeling completely exasperated, I was silenced again by his determination not to listen to me. It was like we were having two separate conversations at the same time and as we wound up back near the flat, passing groups of friends whooping and laughing while heading to the pub, I told him I needed to have something to eat and get ready for work.

That night as I headed out to the hospital to make my 9 p.m. shift, I said everything again. I knew it wasn't a kind thing to do on Christmas Eve but it didn't feel like Christmas for me anyway; I would be working alongside suicidal patients and people who had taken drug overdoses, rather than making my way to midnight mass, singing festive carols and drinking mulled wine. And besides, the message I was trying to get him to hear was hardly a new one.

I was very blunt with Al and just before I closed the heavy door behind me I said again, 'You need to leave. Think about what I've said as I mean every word of it. I want you to move out. I've had enough. There is no discussion. It's over.'

Al stared blankly back at me, as if I would change my mind at any moment and realize I was making some sort of big mistake.

I was relieved to walk away from the flat; it meant we couldn't get into our usual argument that went round and round in a giant circle. But I also felt completely exasperated. I wanted desperately to get my life back on track, and with the inquest out of the way I just needed to escape my toxic relationship with Al.

Please let the message have finally got through to him, I said to myself, wishing with my whole being that he would be gone when I arrived home that evening.

The shift at work was much as I expected. Given the time of year, emotions are always running high; I knew that well enough myself. I saw a couple of suicidal people in A&E, and an older man that the police brought in who was completely psychotic, and I was also called to one of the wards for a slightly more bizarre reason: a man who wouldn't stop hitting himself in the nose, and I tried in vain to get some background documentation on him. It was hectic and demanding and an absolute million miles away from most people's Christmas Eves. I didn't resent it because it was what I had signed up for, but I knew Christmas Day would be a write-off because I'd be so exhausted after such a busy night shift.

In the morning I walked home through the eerily empty streets. The only people I saw were two children whooping with delight as they pedalled shakily along the pavement on what were clearly new bikes, with their parents jogging along behind them red-faced. They had obviously had an early start.

I slotted my key into the front door and wondered what would greet me on the other side, although I had a strong feeling Al would still be there. After all, it was Christmas Day, and I reasoned that he would have trouble finding somewhere else to go. My eyes were heavy with tiredness; I was desperate for some sleep. The best result in my mind was that Al had listened to me and planned to leave after Boxing Day. Maybe we would have some sort of meal together while being civil to one another and that would be that. It wouldn't exactly be the best Christmas Day ever, but it was no doubt the best that could be hoped for under the circumstances.

As I stepped over the threshold of my flat and looked around, I immediately noted that something wasn't right and then quickly clocked that there were no decorations in sight. It was like a blank canvas and looked as if it could belong to somebody else. I did a double take. The colourful, handwritten cards from my friends who are scattered around the country that I had placed around my fireplace had disappeared, along with a small fake Christmas tree, which I had lovingly decorated a few days earlier, and some tinsel that I had put across the mantelpiece and around the television was nowhere to be seen.

'Morning. Happy Christmas,' Al said, coming out of the kitchen. 'I've started cooking.'

It was almost like nothing had happened. I didn't quite know how to react; there were things missing, yet he was talking about turkey and stuffing.

'Where are the Christmas decorations?' I asked.

'I was very angry,' Al replied ruefully.

'Where are they?'

'They're outside in the bin.'

As I was listening to him I then realized that one of my favourite pictures, a painting of two purple butterflies that I had bought down in Cornwall, was missing from the wall, and then I noticed that my medical degree certificate, which had been framed and had also been hanging on the wall, was gone.

'Where's the picture that was on that wall – and my certificate?' I was trying to stay calm, but fatigue and my emotions were getting the better of me. By that point, I couldn't have cared less about the decorations. These items – in particular my certificate – were far more important.

'They are both in the bin,' Al answered.

I stormed outside and looked in the black bin bag and there were all the decorations haphazardly stuffed inside. I picked it up and brought it inside, not caring what else was in the bag, and started digging out all my possessions between the bits of rubbish, food waste and dust. I started finding bits of my medical degree certificate that had been ripped into pieces, and the frame it was in smashed to tiny shards. I completely lost it and just started sobbing. A combination of nervous exhaustion, physical tiredness and anger washed over me. What the hell had he done?

Al was in the kitchen and I ignored him as I went into the bedroom area and sat on the bed, trying to stop the tears from running. No one was hurt, I told myself. The certificate had only been hanging up because there was a spare nail on the wall when I moved in and it wasn't even as if people would notice it coming in. *It's just a piece of paper*, I kept trying to tell myself but even so, it meant years of hard work and sweat; this piece of paper represented everything that was important to me in my career. This man claimed to love me, yet he had destroyed something very, very important to me.

As I gathered my thoughts, there was a small part of me that was hopeful. If he was so vexed, he had obviously thought about us and it must have finally sunk into his head what I wanted and that in my mind at least we were no longer a couple. Whatever this was, maybe it was some sort of progress.

I stamped into the kitchen.

'So you understood what I said then?' I asked.

'Yes.'

'Can we at least be civil today?'

'Yes. I've done us some lunch,' he replied. 'Go and have a sleep. I'll go for a walk now and we can eat later.'

I didn't know what else to do except go to bed. I felt powerless, exhausted and completely numb. I fell into a fitful sleep. When I stirred, the recollection of the morning's events came crashing back to me and I felt another wave of anger and upset. Seconds later, Al came into the room and told me the meal was ready.

We ate in silence, with the television humming in the background providing the only Christmas cheer. I felt really uncomfortable and at that point, I felt so upset about my certificate that I decided if Al was the last person on earth I wouldn't marry him. He repeated over and over: 'I was angry.' He didn't apologize and I couldn't be bothered to point out that he needed to. We were long past that.

After we finished and had cleared the plates away, I told him I was leaving and going home to Aston Abbotts for a few days, which would give him time to find a new home.

I hastily threw some clothes together, drank a strong coffee and hopped into my car. I was at the end of my tether. As I exited Brighton onto the A23 towards the heart of the South Downs, I felt my pulse begin to slow and my mood start to turn towards feeling more optimistic. I told myself that when I came back to the flat, he would be gone. Al had finally accepted it was over and 2011 would bring a fresh start for both of us. God knows I needed it.

It was late when I arrived back at the house and I guess Mum, David and Paul could tell I was in a bad way just by the sight of my face. I barely exchanged a few words with them before I went straight to bed and slept solidly for fourteen hours.

In the morning, over breakfast, I told Mum what had happened and didn't censor the story. I included the fact he had smashed the frame and ripped up my certificate.

She was fuming and told me she was terrified about what Al was capable of. It had never entered her head that I had been trying to end the relationship. I think she thought that if anyone said to their partner they wanted out of the relationship, they would accept it and move out, however hurt or angry they were. She was clearly taking the logical approach, as I had done.

'If he doesn't move out this time, he's not going to go,' she said. 'You've had this conversation again and again. He's just not getting the message.'

I think she was worried that now he had been violent in my home towards my possessions, he could direct his anger at me. After all, we knew he had been threatening towards another human in the past, so why not me? But that thought never even entered my head.

Mum and David suggested involving the police but to me this seemed so extreme. Surely this was just a relationship that wasn't ending well, not a matter for the police? I was still determined to solve the problem by myself and I thought that Al would never touch me. I was confident of that. I wasn't some battered wife who needed police backup. The break-up would soon come to a conclusion.

'This is my relationship. I can sort it out,' I kept saying to them when they urged me to call the police.

My phone buzzed constantly with texts from Al. He had started making excuses about why he couldn't move out.

He wrote: 'It's the Christmas holidays. I'm not going to find a place to stay until the new year now. Can I have some extra time to find somewhere?' and: 'Alison, I've been looking around but nowhere is advertising any rooms. I'll have to wait until January. You can't expect me to just move out in a day. I have quite a lot of stuff to organize.'

I discussed it with the family and we agreed that with a good, well-paid job in London Al should be able to afford to stay in a B&B or a cheap hotel for a few weeks. Despite what he had done, I couldn't help feeling a little bit guilty about kicking him out at that time of year, but they were insistent that I should refuse his request and tell him to be gone by the time I got back.

'When I come home you need to be out,' I typed back. 'You can find a B&B, it won't be hard.'

Mum, David, Paul and I ate meals together, and Paul and I spent a lot of our time sitting together and relaxing in our big front room in front of the fire. He was keen to help so we concocted a backup plan. I would head back to Brighton as planned and, if Al was still there, Paul would come and stay for a few days shortly after and would bring his dog, Linus, with him. We hoped Paul could help turn Al's mind towards leaving and he'd offer his help in looking for a new flat. And having the dog there was always helpful. They could talk 'man to man' over a pint.

In the end I stayed longer at home than I thought I would because Grandpa's funeral was on 30 December. It was held at the nearby Chilterns Crematorium and we all went, along with my Uncle Derek and his wife Irene, their two children and their partners. It was of course a sad affair and everyone shed tears, but we tried to remember the happier times and reflected on what a lovely man he was. David gave an emotional speech and recounted how happy Grandpa had been at the care home in Wing. He recounted tales of Grandpa's famous singing and how he loved to impress the care workers by throwing in the odd French phrase. He recalled how one of Grandpa's favourite jokes was that he started the First World War because he was born in 1914 and how a typical visit would start with our introductory question, 'Are you alright,' to which he would reply, 'No, I am only half right,' and we would all laugh. It was a good send-off.

I drove myself back on New Year's Eve because I was working and, of course, Al was still in the flat. He insisted he needed more time and he couldn't move to a B&B because of all his things. He was talking about leaving but he just didn't do anything or seem to be packing up. I didn't feel desperate because I still thought he would leave in the next few days. That evening after another fairly hectic shift during the day, I stayed in and watched TV blankly on the sofa, while Al sat next to me like a bad smell. At about 11.30 p.m., he suggested we go down to the beach. The thought of being near a bunch of strangers on the beach when it turned midnight seemed better than the alternative, and we walked to the seafront where everyone was letting off their own colourful fireworks and the sky popped with red, blues and greens, while people yelped and hugged each other.

As the clock struck midnight around us people embraced, some passionately kissing, while others just hugged.

Al and I stood apart, our arms folded against our bodies.

'So this year will bring a new start for both of us,' I told him.

'Yes, it will,' Al replied.

A sense of relief washed over me. So, the message had sunk in at long last. He'd had his angry patch, he'd had his stubborn moments and now he was moving on. Or so I thought.

If only it were that easy.

Eight

A Downward Spiral

When I was studying, I learnt about conditions called borderline personality disorder and narcissistic personality disorder, but I don't think I ever really understood what they were as I sat there learning about a lot of complex conditions in a relatively short space of time. Of course, everything is very different in reality to how it is in a textbook full of diagrams, studies and bullet points. However, as I spent my days in the psychiatric hospital with a number of different people displaying strange behaviours, I was starting to catch glimpses of what was involved in these various personality disorders.

Gradually I began to realize that some of Al's behaviour, like the inflated sense of his own importance apparent on his website, the rudeness he had shown to the staff at the health club and his inability to listen to what I was saying whenever I tried to end the relationship, were indicators of some sort of personality disorder. At first, I think I didn't want to make the connection, but as my time in the placement wore on there was no getting away from it.

I remember one woman in particular during my time there, with mad red frizzy hair and a huge mouth, who would come into A&E every night screaming to be admitted to the mental hospital because she was going to kill herself. She had pills, she said, a razor or a rope. We knew being admitted wouldn't solve her problems, but she was clearly so troubled that on occasions she was allowed in. As soon as she was there in the bed, she did everything she could to escape, yelling that she wasn't crazy and she had been banged up against her will, we had forced her there. She wanted to run away and was going to scale the fence.

There was also an overweight young guy who came in regularly, telling us he was an Olympic runner and was set for gold in 2012. He was 'special', he insisted, and people everywhere knew of his sporting gift.

In Al, his narcissistic tendencies were far subtler, and something I only clocked on to a few weeks into my psychiatry placement, but this inability to understand the difference between fantasy and reality was something I was starting to see in him more and more. On some days he was affectionate and sent me constant emails, telling me he loved me, often with a selection of doctor jokes attached; these messages always made me scared as he seemed to have forgotten that the relationship was over. Then at other times he would be boiling over with paranoia and rage, saying my mum had slandered him and we had broken up because of her. He saw things black one day and white the next, there was never anywhere in between.

Many people with personality disorders go through stable periods and I was starting to realize that when Al came over to the UK and we met, life had been on the up for him: he had made it over here without any problems, despite his criminal record (basically he had lied but it had worked); he had landed a great job in London, a city he loved; he was away from the issues of his past and his family; and he was hoping to meet someone and settle down. But as soon as things hadn't gone quite his way or as smoothly as he wanted, this other side to him started coming out. He felt the need to boast about achievements and talked constantly about how much we loved one another and that we were still getting married.

During the first weekend in January, with Al still refusing to move out of the flat, our new action plan came into force and Paul came down with the idea of him spending three or four days with me to give Al a kick up the backside.

By then, of course, Al was staying on the sofa – although he complained constantly about his back – but he still refused to move out.

Paul arrived on the Friday and took Al for a walk and a drink at the pub and tried to tell him that I wasn't interested anymore and that he needed to move on. Paul told me that Al had been quite happy to discuss everything with him and seemed to accept that he needed to leave, agreeing to do so that weekend. I don't know what changed but by the time he came back he was telling me Paul needed to stay in a B&B.

'This is my home,' Al ranted. 'He needs to get out. He's interfering. I've paid rent!'

'No, Paul is my family. He has come to stay with me and spend time with me,' I told him. 'You need to move out.'

'No, I won't! This is my home!'

I could tell Paul was having to work very hard to control himself and not hit Al and, in the end, after I insisted I would talk more with Al by myself, Paul dragged the blow-up bed, a pillow and his sleeping bag into the corridor between the kitchen and bathroom area and set himself up there with Linus at his feet. For most people this would be a pretty uncomfortable set-up, but given Paul's bohemian lifestyle this was probably the norm.

In the bedroom area I tried to get through to Al again and repeated myself for what felt like the hundredth time, insisting that he must remove himself from the flat. Again, it was futile and in the end I was so exasperated and maddened by his stubbornness that I just gave up and went to bed.

In the morning, when we were all eating breakfast in an awkward silence, me feeling very uncomfortable and Paul and Al glaring at each other across the table, there was a loud banging on the door. Paul had spoken to David the night before, filling him in on what had been going on, and David had called his local police to ask for advice on what to do when someone wouldn't move out of a property. His local station had eventually contacted the Sussex police force, who said they would come round to the flat to check that everyone was OK, especially given Al's history of violence. But Mum and David's fear was that I would, under pressure from

Al, say that everything was fine and that I hadn't asked him to leave. So unbeknown to me, a very nervous Mum and David had also got in the car and were making their way down to Brighton. Their patience was obviously at an end and they had decided that if I wasn't going to act then they certainly were.

As I opened my front door I was pretty shocked to see two smart and youngish policemen standing there with their helmets in hand. When they asked what was going on, I told them nothing and that we were 'having a bit of a domestic'. I figured that they must see this kind of stuff all the time and it must seem like a complete waste of time. To be totally truthful, I felt a bit silly.

When Al clocked them, he was immediately furious and turned on me, his eyes burning, 'You rang the police, Alison! Why did you call the police?'

'I didn't,' I responded. 'I didn't call them. I don't know who did.'

He spat back, 'You did! You called them!'

One of the policemen interrupted him, 'Excuse me. What is going on?'

'The relationship has ended but my ex won't move out,' I told them.

'Whose name is on the rental agreement?'

'It's in my name,' I told them.

'She did that on purpose! She never wanted my name to be on there!' Al raved.

One of the policemen ushered me into the corridor outside the flat to talk more, while the other one stayed with Al and Paul, who by then were having a full-blown altercation. The policeman was telling Al that if the relationship was over and it was my name that was on the contract then he had no right to stay there, and he was also urging Paul to stay calm, while acknowledging that he could tell he was trying to help me.

The man I was talking to was kind and understanding, but repeated what I already knew. It was a fairly short-lived conversation and as they left they told me to call them whenever I wanted if I was worried about anything. As the policeman I had been speaking to walked out he made the hand gesture of a phone at his ear with his thumb and little finger and mouthed, 'Call us.'

Right, this is my moment, I thought to myself. This was the moment it was finally going to happen. Turning back, I said to Al, 'Pack your bags. I'm going to go for a walk with Paul to clear my head. We were happy once but we're not anymore. It's over and I want you gone. I don't want to find you here when we get back.'

Al just sat there on the bed blankly staring at the wall as I said goodbye.

'Please post the key through the door on your way out,' I said, before turning and closing the door behind me.

As Paul and I were walking down the road, my mobile phone rang. It was Mum, telling me they were on their way down. We agreed to meet them at the Wetherspoon's on the marina. I wanted to give Al time to pack and leave and I thought we'd had enough drama for one morning.

As we nursed our drinks at the pub we filled Mum and

David in on what had happened with the police. David and Paul agreed to go back to the flat, while Mum and I stayed in the pub, just in case Al was still lingering. They took my keys so they could let themselves in.

The whole thing was horrible. I hated doing that to him. It felt absurd and extreme to boot him out forcefully kicking and screaming, but everyone kept telling me that if he hadn't gone by then, he wasn't ever planning to leave. I would be stuck with him forever.

I found out from them later what happened. Paul went in first because Al would be expecting him back and David followed with Linus on his chain lead.

'Are you still here?' David asked.

'Where is Alison?' Al said, clearly surprised to see him.

'She's safe,' David replied. By that point they were convinced he was dangerous and a threat to me.

He added, 'Mr Dhalla, you have two choices. Either you pack your bags and leave now of your own accord or I make a call and the two policemen who visited you this morning will come and help you to leave.'

Whether that would ever have happened is questionable – I think the police had done as much as they could at that point – but I think David was going to say whatever it took to get him out.

David had asked Paul to stand between Al and the kitchen and he stood in front of the fireplace with Linus at his feet.

'What, you want me to leave now?' Al asked.

'Yes, right now.'

'But I might not be able to find anywhere to stay,' he said.

'That didn't seem to be a problem when you demanded Paul leave the flat earlier.'

'I have paid rent,' he said.

'Tough,' David replied.

Al was clearly annoyed but reluctantly began thrusting things into various bags, holdalls and boxes. Paul called a taxi and after being asked for his keys a couple of times, Al opened his briefcase to retrieve them and fumbled to get them off the ring. After a short wait, a taxi pulled up, Paul handed over a twenty-pound note and Al was gone. Finally.

When I saw them come back into the pub smiling and giving a thumbs up, we all breathed a huge sigh of relief and ordered ourselves a round of stiff drinks.

Paul and David stayed in the flat that first night after Al left, while Mum and I checked into the nearby Premier Inn. By then I understood that if Al got his foot through the door again, we would be back to square one, so I was relieved that they had agreed to stay there. While David had to go back to work, Mum remained with me for the next few days and Paul, before he left with Linus, had managed to find a hardware shop and got a new lock barrel for the inner door of the flat. The outer door was shared with other tenants so could not be changed.

Finally everyone would move on with their lives.

The first thing I did was to give the place a good clean. I thought if I scrubbed the flat from top to bottom, all traces of Al would be gone. I wanted to restore it to how it was before he had been there. I wanted to rewrite him out of my time in

Brighton and this seemed like a good first step. I spent a whole morning dusting, hoovering, spraying and wiping. I stripped my bed and threw all the covers into the washer, along with all my towels. I felt great afterwards – red-faced and sweating but still somehow cleansed.

Then I turned my attention to sorting out the mound of paperwork that lived on my dining table. As I sorted through my possessions, it became clear that Al had taken some of my personal belongings. As I went to find my travel insurance, I discovered my identification documents including my passport, driving licence and birth certificate were all missing. It was a moment of absolute shock and disbelief. My skin prickled uncomfortably. I sat there looking through my files again and again and again, hoping and silently pleading that maybe I had just missed them, maybe they were in another safe place, maybe I had made some sort of mistake, until it finally sank in that I actually had no identification. Mum and I had been talking about going to Thailand in February, now the inquest was over and Al had left. Looking back, at the time, I was more worried about not being able to leave the country to go on holiday than I was about the paperwork, even though I knew it was going to be a pain to replace everything. It was only later down the line that I began to realize that if you really want to destroy a person, if you really want revenge, then that is the way to go about it. He knew that eventually it would hit me on a deeply emotional level; it would be as if I had never existed.

However, if it meant that was the end of it with Al, I could replace those things and carry on. It could be sorted, however time-consuming it would be to sit on phone lines where irritating jingles plinked in the background along with recorded messages about how important my call was. It was a small price to pay. I felt quite defiant then; if he thought he'd wreaked some sort of revenge then he was wrong. I was still winning.

Then the letters started.

Nine

Poison Pen

For a few days my phone was eerily quiet. It stopped buzzing incessantly, the text messages stopped and unusually I was opening up my emails and there were none from Al.

I felt very uneasy about his sudden lack of contact. I was delighted that he was leaving me alone but I knew it was very unlike him. By this point I was in such a stressed mindset that, even with him gone, I couldn't stop thinking about him. Still, I hoped he had finally got the message. David had told him that if he got in touch we would call the police so I actually thought for a few days that he might listen for once. Now we all knew he had previous convictions and a criminal record, we would use it against him if he overstepped the mark, and he knew that. I imagined that this would act as a big deterrent.

However, the week after we got him out of the flat it soon became all too clear that, far from moving on, he was intent on destroying my reputation. He wanted to make me sit up and listen in any way he could.

Al had left on a Saturday, and the following Thursday morning I was on the psychiatry ward doing my daily jobs when my consultant walked over and asked quite formally to 'have a word'. My heart flipped and started banging desperately against my ribcage; surely I hadn't done something wrong? I had only just put the inquest behind me and had been so thorough, so careful with everything. I started thinking back over what I had done, which patients I had seen and any problem cases, rolling them back in my head like some sort of Rolodex organizer. Was it something to do with the girl with bipolar who had shouted at me? Or the family of the man who was sectioned against his will? I had played everything with a straight bat, done my job and moved on.

The consultant led me in silence into a manager's office, where he shut the door firmly behind me. A middle-aged lady dressed in a grey suit and heavy, thick-rimmed glasses sat opposite. She wasn't someone I had met before but I knew she was part of the senior management team because I had seen her walking purposefully around the hospital with her identification around her neck. She gave a half-smile but I could tell that whatever this conversation was about, it was something serious.

'Please sit down,' she said.

OK, so we were going to be there for a while, I thought, as I gingerly pulled the plastic chair towards me and sat, nervously, still scraping around in my mind for what they could want to talk to me about.

'We have received a letter and we are concerned about it – and about you, Alison,' she said.

'OK.' I replied. I was flummoxed. *A letter from who? About what?*

'I'll show you the start,' she said and flipped the piece of A4 white paper round to face me. I started reading and I knew immediately that Al had sent it.

He made two accusations: firstly, that I had murdered the patient at the hospice and, secondly, that I had stolen drugs from the NHS for my own use and to sell on to my brother Paul.

I was shocked into silence and I could feel my heart hammering in my ears as my face and neck shone red with embarrassment and outrage.

'I know you've been working here for over a month now and we're worried that a patient has got hold of details and has managed to find out a lot of personal information about you,' she explained. 'Could that be the case? Can you think who might have written this?'

I breathed a huge sigh of relief. I figured that working in a psychiatric unit wasn't a bad place to be then because they could tell immediately that the letter writer was unstable.

'No, this is from my ex-boyfriend,' I responded quietly. 'We've just been through a difficult break-up and he hasn't taken it very well.'

'Oh, er . . . wow,' she responded, clearly not having dealt

with anything like this before. 'Do you think he could be unwell, I mean, mentally unstable?'

'Yes, I think he might be,' I replied. This was the first time I had voiced to anyone that I thought Al could be a bit crazy.

I didn't want to say too much. I knew from my experience with the inquest that the less I said at this stage, the better. Al's mention of the inquest was fine, of course, as I had been exonerated in court – although I had hoped to put it behind me – but it was the accusation that I had stolen drugs that was the strongest charge and potentially a sackable offence.

'Right, well, the fact we have received the letter means that we can't ignore it and we will have to investigate further because this is a serious allegation. We'll have to inform various members of the management team and you'll need to talk to them further about this, I'm afraid.'

She looked at me and I could recognize the look of pity in her eyes. I was determined not to cry, or even let my eyes fill up with salty tears. I knew I had to keep going to show people I could cope. Whatever had happened in my personal life, it wouldn't roll over into my working life. I couldn't let it.

As I walked back to the ward, knowing that I had to get through the rest of the day, my shock turned to fury and embarrassment.

How dare he? I thought. This was a man who claimed to love me, yet he had started a mini-vendetta against me. This was another way that he hoped to control me and it was just another reminder of the lengths he was prepared to go to to do that.

Over the next few days I discovered that this letter was

sent not just to the hospital I was working at then. It had gone all around Brighton: Al had sent copies to other senior doctors at the hospital, one to the coroner, a number to the palliative care team and a few to the GP's surgery where I had done my previous placements. Various managers called me and explained that they had received the note. This was the scary thing: he knew my life inside out. If my reputation wasn't already in tatters after the inquest, goodness knows what people would think after this. I wanted to shrivel up and disappear.

None of the family were left unscathed by Al's poison pen. My mum's neighbours had contacted her, informing her they had received an anonymous letter through the door. It seems he had also taken it upon himself to write a letter about Mum and David and had posted it through every letterbox in the village. They were equally appalled and embarrassed, although most of the neighbours knew them well enough to know that none of it was true.

The letter restated the accusations against me that had been in the letter to my employers. It was also particularly vicious towards Paul, presumably because of his part in evicting Al from my flat. Some of the accusations made against him were serious but others made us laugh out loud. Even Linus was the subject of a character assassination. The letter accused Paul of 'Use of a weapon (i.e. a dog)', 'causing bodily harm', and 'hunting in the off season/hunting without a licence'. Linus has never caused anyone harm and Paul is not a hunter. The letter concluded with the warning, 'Mr Paul

Hewitt is armed (rifle, metal tools, large dog known to bite) and may be considered dangerous. Approach with caution. Thank you.'

Another letter followed to David's employers, laying out a further list of farcical so-called crimes, committed by David himself and Paul, before describing them physically and listing their contact details. He accused Mum of all sorts of horrible things, including not burying Grandpa properly.

'This would be considered "Illegal Possession of a Human Corpse" and "Conducting Indignity to Human Remains",' he wrote.

He also accused her of driving Dad 'into an early grave', and of only marrying David when she did to maximize Dad's pension. He added that she was likely to be suffering from 'narcissism' and 'Black Widow Syndrome'.

He didn't sign the one to the neighbours or the one to my employers but because it used identical text to the one he sent to David's work, which he did sign, it was evident to the police who the culprit was.

I found the poison pen letters so preposterous that it was hard to believe it was happening. It was so difficult for me to read them; they were so horrible, so manipulative and, in some cases, so laughable, that they were just really disturbing. Why would anyone want to read them? Would anyone really believe what they said? What would people be saying about us?

Mum and David were disturbed, embarrassed and angry in equal measures. Everything he wrote was just plain horrible lies. Everyone in the village would be talking about it over cups of tea, games of bridge and flower arranging. There was absolutely no doubt about that.

Mum and David took a pragmatic approach and informed their local police, asking their neighbours to pass on the letters and handle them as little as possible. The police took statements and told them they would investigate.

Of course both David and I became embroiled in workplace investigations. I didn't really know where to start and I certainly didn't have a plan about how I would deal with it. I started by calling my medical insurers. I think they were left equally flummoxed by what to do but instructed me as best they could and told me to get back in touch as the investigation unfolded at the hospital.

It was then that I knew I would have to go to the police and talk to them about what had happened and how Al had behaved. I didn't really feel like I had a choice. I had waited until then because I knew there was an awful lot more at stake for Al if he was known to the police here, including his visa and his job in the UK, and I kept deluding myself into thinking he would get the message and move on. Again, it might have been misguided but at this time, even after the letters, I never once wanted him to end up being thrown out the country, jobless or homeless. I was very angry but I never wanted his life as he knew it to be over, whatever ills he wished for me or my family. But unfortunately he had now forced my hand. He had taken things one step too far this time.

I trudged down to Brighton police station and gave a statement to one of the officers on duty. They agreed that he sounded aggrieved by the breakdown of the relationship and hopefully everything would blow over after that. Al knew that he had hit me where it hurt most – at work, where I spent most of my time and energy trying to build a career, and with the destruction of my personal documents. I prayed that he didn't have any more bright ideas up his sleeve in some sort of attempt to make me feel as wretched as he clearly hoped I would.

The young police officer, who looked quite junior, told me she thought Al sounded like an angry ex-lover and that it would most likely all blow over soon enough. She told me to come back and see them if he did anything else, as it would be possible to get an injunction out against him should the situation worsen. They didn't have any advice for me about how to handle someone like Al and I felt left on my own to cope. As they said the word 'worsen' an uneasy feeling sat in my gut. How could it get worse than that?

At the start of February I went on a much-needed holiday to Phuket in Thailand with Mum. I had organized a day off work and paid an extra fee to get an emergency passport. Throughout my time working in A&E, then the inquest and then the drama with Al, I was living for my holidays. They somehow gave me the energy and space I needed to deal with my everyday life once I returned home. David couldn't take the time off work so remained at home but my brothers, their respective other halves and my nephews came out at some point for different amounts of time. The idea of the holiday was to put everything that had happened behind us, and while the emails and letters were still there in the back of our minds, we thought we could have some time together and mark an end in what had been a hellish ordeal all round. Mum paid for us all to go; I think she felt that we needed to come together as a family and show me how much support I had, and I felt really looked after and happy to see them all.

It was good to escape Brighton, be away from work and give myself a bit of distance from the break-up and letters. The location was beautiful, all warm white sand, crystal-clear emerald sea and palm trees. The hotel resort was incredible too, with every comfort you can imagine, and we spent most of our time being big kids, clowning around in the swimming pools with my nephews. I also had Thai massages every day, when a tiny Thai woman clicked and bent me back into shape. By the end of my two weeks away, I really began to feel like myself again. I knew I still had some serious discussions to have at work but, in the main, I could move on with my life.

But at the beginning of February, while I was still away, I started to receive phone calls and texts from Al again. Bizarrely he talked to me like he had never sent the letters and accused me of murder. He spoke at length about himself, telling me that he had moved back to London, had found a new job and home and was getting on with things. He told me mundane stuff like how he had eaten three bananas one morning and he sometimes reminisced about the early days of the relationship. I didn't respond to anything he said or did and just tried to pretend it wasn't happening. I ignored his calls but he continued ringing until I could stand it no more, and I eventually caved in and spoke to him. As I picked up, he would beg for five minutes of my time. He often sent me emails too, and would sign off 'your fiancé' or use a nickname I had for him, 'Al the Pal.'

There were lovey-dovey emails, which read like this one:

I am sorry that I lied to you about certain things, Alison. I love you very much, Alison. I was either scared or trying to protect you, but I told you everything, Alison. You are the only person I trust, Alison. Please let me into your life again, please. You mean the world to me, Alison. You are my true love, my soul mate, Alison. I miss you so much, sweetie.

He also bombarded Mum with ridiculous emails, along these lines:

Besides cooking, I make tea for Alison everyday, Pam. Alison likes her tea with the tea bag out quickly, so weak, with some milk. For breakfast, I usually buy yoghurt for us, fruit juice – Alison likes pineapple juice – and fruit such as bananas, apples, honeydew melon and cantaloupe. On the weekends, I make Alison either eggie toast (French toast) or an egg omelette with onions, green peppers, pepper and cheese. Usually I burn the omelette and eggie toast because I want to make sure it is well cooked, so we open the windows and door to let out the smoke and smell. On the weekends, I will cook Alison a delicious healthy dinner such as salmon, which we get from Asda in the tin-foil wrapper, vegetables and pudding. Although Alison told me not to make or buy pudding anymore because she wants to lose some weight. I told Alison that I think she is beautiful, and she is to me. I love Alison very much.

Shortly after my return from Thailand, envelopes started falling through the letterbox, just one or two each day posted from London. I could recognize his writing immediately. Some I opened and others I just didn't bother with. They were much the same as the texts and emails, harking back to the time we had spent together. He repeatedly told me he loved me and wanted us to be together. Some days I got back from the hospital to four or five letters sitting on the doorstep, with Al's handwriting on the envelopes. Towards the end of the relationship he had told me that his contract with RSA was up – it later transpired that he was sacked, but I'll never know the true details of what happened. He told me he was working on a temporary basis at a Korean bank, or at least that is what I gathered from the few letters I glanced at. All of these letters, texts and emails were again a sign of him attempting to control me and while on the face of it most of them seemed pretty harmless, just receiving them was stressful. Each time I opened my inbox or my phone beeped, I would feel a lurch of panic because I knew it would be him trying to contact me.

I would collect the letters over the space of two weeks and drop them in at the police station. I felt a bit stupid doing it because they were just love letters and I was pretty sure they'd end up in the bin at some point but in hindsight I'm so glad I did it.

The idea that I was being stalked simply never entered my mind. Stalkers were people obsessed with celebrities who followed them around begging for autographs, weren't they? Or hangers-on who dressed up as gardeners or waitresses at parties and tried to enter the homes of their idols? The stumbling block in my mind was that I thought stalkers were anonymous and had some sort of imaginary connection with the stalkee. Also, the phrase had become almost slang for me by that point. When we were at uni one of my female friends was followed around by this guy who was doing her chemistry course, who had buck teeth and bad breath, asking for help with his coursework or lecture notes. We actually nicknamed him 'Stalker'. I still somehow thought that what I was going through with Al was just a bad break-up. A very, very bad break-up.

The police, of course, viewed what was happening as a domestic dispute and, like me, thought – and hoped – that it would just blow over. Before the two new stalking laws were passed in 2012, a stalker's behaviour was dealt with under the previous harassment laws, but I think this made it difficult to clearly identify the type of crime that had been committed. Stalkers were viewed as rejected lovers rather than criminals and often remained invisible. Of course, every telltale signal that he was a stalker was there.

What I know now was that rather than living in London and finding himself a new flat, like he'd said, Al had rented a flat almost opposite mine on the corner of the next street so he would be able to watch me walking to and from work and going in and out of my flat. Later it was revealed that he had rented it for three months from January to March so he was living and breathing my every move during that time.

It also emerged much later that he had hired his own private investigator to follow me around the clock over the course of two weekends, to monitor my every move and see where and who I'd been out with – and in particular, if I'd been with another man. Al had demanded video surveillance and paid £1,800 in cash for the job. The private investigator who he had hired claimed that he didn't think there was anything out of the ordinary about the job, until Al asked him to knock on my door and pretend to be conducting a survey for a women's magazine and ask me if I'd had sex in the last two months. The investigator refused, thinking the request was preposterous. Al also asked him to investigate David, saying that he had been involved with prostitutes. Even to the PI, who knew nothing of the situation, it was obvious Al was determined to bring Mum and David down and again he drew the line at this. This guy was the only person who knew where Al lived at the time, beside the landlord, and afterwards he said that he thought it was extremely weird that someone would want to be so near to their ex. So, having no job and living so close to where I was, meant that Al would spend his days following my movements, writing emails to me and my family and becoming more and more manic, hell-bent on either getting me back, or getting some sort of sick revenge.

I think by this point he had realized that I was never going to take him back, so in his mind that left him only one course of action. He was after me.

By the middle of February, the emails seemed to be coming thicker and faster than ever and would pop up on my screen multiple times a day to my various personal email addresses. That was one thing, but I got the biggest shock one day when

I was at work, going through some official stuff, and his name popped into my work email. I don't know how he got my address, although I imagine they are not too hard to find out, but it completely floored me. When I was at work, I was managing to forget about the harassment. I felt that it was my safe haven and I could leave my bleeping phone in my bag, and forget about the postman with his heavy sack, while I got on with a job that really mattered. It shook me up a lot. I think it was then that I realized there was no escaping him.

The letters and the emails continued and I was introduced to a liaison officer, Emily, with long brown hair, freckly skin and a wide smile, and she became my point of contact at the police station. I would drive over there on my way to work and hand in anything Al had sent me and she would pop up, smiling, asking, 'Another batch?' She became like a friend who I had a good gossip with and sometimes in the later stages she'd come round to the flat, make herself a cup of tea and we'd get whatever needed to be done out of the way.

On two occasions he forwarded me emails from a new dating agency he had joined, presumably in an attempt to make me jealous and beg for him to come back, and another time he promised me he was leaving the country and that I would never hear from him again. He wrote:

> **I have not touched any of your belongings (neither taken nor destroyed), nor have I sent any letters, nor have I telephoned anybody. Please stop trying to frame me and accuse me of things, stop harassing me Alison!!! I have already packed my belongings and the taxi will be here shortly to take me to my flight; I am leaving the UK this morning, good-bye.**

After reading that I guessed the police had been in touch with him to try and deter him, but it clearly hadn't worked, and of course the claims about moving away were far too good to be true, as two days later he sent an email begging for us to go and stay at a B&B in Arundel and stop at one of the pubs I liked called the Crown & Anchor.

Most of the emails were pleading, frenzied and hysterical. They would read something like this one:

> My dearest Alison, I love you so much. It has been hell living without you. I miss you so so much sweetie. There is not one day that goes by where I do not think of you. I cry almost every day, particularly in the evenings. Last weekend I cried all day on Saturday, which was supposed to be our wedding day, and then on Monday – Valentine's Day – I cried so badly because I wanted to be with you, Alison. I wanted to post you a Valentine's Day card, but I was scared. Please do not tell your mother that I have contacted you. Our relationship is between you and me, nobody else. You love me too, Alison. You wanted to marry me. You wanted to have children with me and planned our future together. We were going to live in a house near a train service into London and then you were going to work as a GP in whatever local hospital there was . . . You are my soulmate, Alison, I cannot live without you. You are my dream girl – you are kind, understanding, funny, I think you are beautiful, Alison. I love your smile, your face, your eyes, your personality and your voice – I love everything about you, Alison. I love you so much, Alison, so, so much. I feel so drained and tired. You are my life, Alison. We were together for over a year, we lived together for almost a year and we love each other. Please, please do not throw our relationship away, Alison. I feel like

> my heart has been ripped out. I am sobbing my eyes out
> right now as I am typing. Last Sunday I woke up and visual-
> ized you beside me and me saying to you, 'Wake up, Mrs
> Alison Dhalla. Wake up, my sweetheart', then I realized you
> were no longer here and I cried. We were and are so happy
> when we are together, Alison. I miss walking with you down
> by the beach, walking into town and around the Lanes,
> drinking wheat-grass shots and eating at Choccywoccydoo-
> dah. I miss bringing you sushi and ordering Thai food for us.
> I miss watching *Poirot* with you on the sofa and holding you
> in my arms, Alison. I miss you so much, Alison. Please,
> please. I am yours, Alison. I have always been yours and I
> have loved you from the first day we met and my love for you
> has grown and grown. I love you more than life, Alison,
> more than anything in the world.

I was hoping naively that if I ignored him, he would go away.
The days rattled past and I was succeeding in ignoring most
of his constant pestering but then something small would
happen, like he would use up all of my voicemail tape so
none of my friends could leave messages or he would ring
throughout the night and wake me up so I was groggy and
exhausted the next day when I was on duty and I would cry
tears of frustration. He made me feel so helpless and powerless. I didn't turn my phone off because I refused to allow him
to force me to cut myself off from the rest of the world.
Family and friends urged me to throw my phone into the sea,
or in a bin and get a new one. But I knew that he would just
find other ways to get to me; he'd somehow find out any new
number I had or send more emails because he couldn't phone
me. He was clearly still determined to show that he could

infiltrate my life, whatever course of action I took. He had locked himself into some sort of relationship with me, against my will, and I was frightened. I also didn't take their advice because I wanted to know when he had finally moved on and would leave me alone, so I could live my life again. The only way I would know this for sure would be if the constant emails, texts and phone calls stopped. So I would wipe away the tears, pick myself up and carry on, hoping that the following day would bring an end to my misery.

During this time the work investigation was ongoing, giving me another constant reminder of how Al had infiltrated my life. I was introduced to a few managers and was questioned by some senior people at the hospital. It seemed to come to a conclusion during one of these interviews where the staff member tried to go into detail with me about what Al had said. He asked me why Al would make something like this up and I was forced to explain the situation. I answered his questions but I was aware that if it was going to escalate, I would need to have a legal representative present. However, I was reluctant to reveal the extent of the problems between Al and me. The allegations Al was making were serious, but I answered their questions honestly and the management team realized that I had done nothing wrong. I think they just needed to satisfy themselves that it had been dealt with correctly but I felt humiliated and horribly exposed. Every time I managed to pick myself up, he seemed to somehow knock me back down again. I wondered if I would ever be more than just a thin shell of the person I was before I met him.

Ten

Cross-fire

Sunday 20 March 2011 started out as a normal day. I had dragged myself out of bed, showered and changed and was leaving the house for work when Al appeared at my front door. He had clearly been sitting in the porch area waiting for me for some time. I immediately felt a lurch of adrenaline and I hoped that the shock didn't register in my face.

'You've been sending a lot of texts,' I said.

'I just wanted to see you,' Al answered, smiling.

'Look Al, I'm busy.'

'Can we just talk?'

'Well, I'm going to work. You can walk with me but after that, it's done. I'm not talking about this anymore.'

In a rather perverse way, a small part of me was pleased to see him, so I could tell him face-to-face just how infuriated I was about the letters and what the consequences had been and how they had made me feel. I wanted to tell him that if he wanted to destroy my reputation he had given it a pretty good go.

As we walked, I let Al talk first; whatever he needed to say I just wanted him to say it and then leave me alone. He started off by filling me in about his new life in London – more of the same things that filled his dreary letters and repetitive emails. Perhaps in some attempt to make me feel guilty, he explained that he had pawned back the engagement ring for far less than he bought it for. He missed me, he said, and he needed more answers about what went wrong and why I had felt the need to finish it.

When it finally seemed like he had got whatever he needed to out of his system, I started my rant.

'Do you realize what you have done to me at work?' I told him. 'I am going through investigations with managers at the hospital! Are you trying to destroy my career? After everything that happened at the inquest, what on earth were you thinking? Why would you write such horrible and manipulative lies?'

The severity of what I was saying didn't seem to register and all he could say was, 'I was hurt.'

I knew he was selfish, childish and single-minded, but I still thought there must be part of the polite and enthusiastic Al I used to know in there somewhere who would see reason and logic in what I was trying to tell him.

I continued, 'I had to sit down with some really senior staff members and explain myself because of your letter—'

'It's behind us now,' he said, putting his hands on my

shoulders and stepping in closer to me, a sickly sweet smile on his face. 'I love you, Alison.'

'No, Al, it's not behind us! And I don't love you!' I said, stepping out of his grip. 'I don't think you realize quite what you have done and the consequences of your actions. After that, why would I want to see you?'

'I just want us to be friends, Alison. I want us to be civil to each other and to remain friends.'

'No, Al, you don't seem to get this. This is serious. You accused me of stealing!'

'But I was angry. Can we meet up again to talk more?'

I was completely exasperated. I didn't have a clue how to get rid of him. 'No, we can't Al. I don't want to. It's over.'

'Can I wait for you? I want to talk to you more. I can walk home with you?'

My shoulders slumped in defeat as I realized that the only way I would be able to get rid of him was if I agreed that we could talk some more.

'If you want to wait, that's up to you,' I said, sighing deeply.

When I finished my shift, of course, Al was standing in the entrance of the hospital by the doors and he jumped up as he saw me.

We strolled back to the flat slowly, stopping at the park nearby for a few minutes where we sat on a damp bench as children on bikes rode past and dog walkers threw balls.

I repeated what I had said earlier in the day and went through what the consequences of the letters had been, step-by-step, trying to ram home how horrible they had been. I didn't want him to get away with it and not realize what he had done; I wanted to pass on just some of the stress, anguish and humiliation. Al clearly also felt he had some things to offload; he played up the fact he was hurt by my actions and how he truly thought that I had wanted to marry him. When we seemed to be going back over old ground I told him I was leaving. I hoped the talk had been cathartic for both of us and would be the conversation that he needed to put whatever he felt to bed.

Finally, before he went off to the train station, I issued him with a choice: if he stopped calling and emailing my family, I would speak to him once a week. I still thought that if I handled him carefully I could keep the situation in check. It would get my family off my back and would satisfy Al, I hoped, until he finally started to feel better about the break-up and even, perhaps, met someone else. It was just a matter of time.

After that day the phone calls and emails to my family did stop but it was in direct proportion to how much he called, texted and emailed me. Al started aggressively demanding my attention every day. When I let his calls ring out, he would leave ranting voicemails asking me why I hadn't picked up and telling me that I had made an agreement with him to keep in touch.

'Why did you lie to me?' he would yell. 'You promised me that you'd speak to me! You are not sticking to our agreement.'

Al turned up twice more on my doorstep. The first time he looked like he had come straight from work and was wearing a suit. I was once again floored by his presence. I knew that if

I let him inside it would be game over and he would never leave again.

'What are you doing here, Al?' I sighed. I had started treating him like a child who constantly did the wrong thing, yet never learned.

'I've got your favourite: sushi,' he said, gesturing towards a bag he was carrying. 'There's salmon nigiri and cucumber maki. Will you let me in so we can eat it together?'

'No,' I said, slamming the door in his face.

He knocked continuously for ten minutes while I tried to work out what the hell to do. I couldn't let him in but the only way I could get him to leave would be to spend some time with him, so I told him I'd walk round the block.

'I'm not eating with you,' I tried to tell him. 'We're not in a relationship. I don't want to have dinner with you.'

'But it's your favourite; it's sushi. I've come all the way from London to give it to you. I bought it especially from your favourite place in Victoria.'

'No, Al.'

What was going on in his head I don't know, but I eventually persuaded him to leave and he got on a bus, presumably pretending to go back to the train station. I was fast learning that the only way he would leave me was if I postponed talking to him or seeing him and I think on that occasion I agreed to talk to him later that day. Otherwise he would just keep calling me or not leave my side. It was continuous. I didn't tell the police about this encounter at the time, praying that it would be the last time it happened.

*

As was now apparent from his actions towards me, Al seemed to cling on to anything he could and had a habit of becoming fixated by things. One of the people outside of the family who he became obsessed by was Nick. Nick is very creative and runs his own web design business, and one day Al phoned him, pretending to be a potential client and telling him that he had some web design projects that needed doing. Could they meet up and discuss it further? I had told Nick a bit about Al when we had met back in November and he no doubt had been filled in on the whole situation via his mum since the letters had arrived on the mats of the neighbours. When he clocked Al's Canadian voice, he took his number and told him he would call back. After relaying his suspicions to his mum, Claire, he decided it sounded very much like something Al would do so he made the decision not to return the call. However, Al was persistent and called back a number of times. Nick picked up once, not recognizing the number. When he started talking about Nick's ex-wife, Nick said he knew it was Al. Nick's new girlfriend was called Melissa, but I didn't know the name of his first wife, so couldn't have mentioned it. It became clear Al had gone up to London and gone through the marriage certificates because he seemed to know all about her and started talking about her and their two children. Nick was understandably freaked out and hung up as quickly as he could, dialling 1471 to retrieve his number. He passed the message on to his mum, Claire, who in turn told Mum, who let the police know. After finding out about this, I went to the police again to try to obtain an injunction, but it wasn't possible because I needed to know where Al was living and despite trying to find out, Al was evasive.

Another disturbing turn of events that occurred around that time concerned two of my friends, Abi and Ed, who were getting married later in the year. They were both in my year group at Warwick University where I had done my medicine degree, and we had all bonded over the highs and lows of trying to gain a huge amount of knowledge in a relatively short space of time and pass our exams. They still lived in Leamington Spa and I saw them about once a year, when all my group of uni pals would converge at someone's house or flat and catch up. We hadn't seen each other for a while; we were registrar doctors doing placements all over the country so finding time when we were all free was proving impossible.

Al knew that I had been invited to Abi and Ed's wedding and had received my invitation, and he kept asking if he could go with me. He must have remembered from the save-the-date card that had been stuck on my fridge that it was taking place at a hotel in Stratford-upon-Avon.

The next thing I knew I had Abi on the phone, telling me she couldn't talk for long because she was racing to make it to a shift at the hospital where she was working, but something strange had happened.

'Alison, do you know someone called Al?'

'Erm, yes.'

'Well, he's just turned up here on my doorstep and he's got loads of pictures of you together,' she continued. 'He seems very nice but he keeps asking to come to the wedding. It's a bit strange that he's turned up here, on my doorstep . . .'

Al was showing his shrewd and resourceful side; he had also worked out their address.

'Oh no, I'm so sorry! Please, Abi, I don't want him at the wedding,' I replied. 'I will be there but on my own. Listen, the Al thing . . . it's a long story . . .'

I promised her that I would fill her in properly about Al and what had happened when I next saw her and she rushed off to work.

I was furious and immediately dialled Al's number. I could hear he was on the train from the muffled chatter in the background. Presumably he was making his way back from Warwick on the train.

'Where are you?' I demanded.

'I've just done something,' he replied.

'Yes, you've just been to Abi and Ed's house, asking to be invited to the wedding, haven't you?'

'How do you know?'

'Because she just called me,' I said.

'It was supposed to be a romantic surprise,' he answered. 'I wanted to book us a room together. There is room at the ceremony and then the reception, they told me, and they are happy for me to come.'

'You think I'd go away with you, or sleep in the same bed as you, after everything that's happened?'

'No, that's fine,' Al said. 'I can sleep on the sofa. You can have the bed. I just wanted to spend time with you. It will be really roman—'

I was so angry, I simply jabbed my finger at the 'end call'

button and hung up. It was like I was talking to a big, fat brick wall.

A few days later on a Friday at around 8 p.m. in the evening there was a knock at the door. I did think it was a bit strange because I wasn't expecting anyone but figured it could be the neighbour with some post or the landlord checking in. Of course, it was Al and as soon as I saw him I told him I was working the next day and slammed the door. It rattled on the hinges with the force.

Just as my heart was slowing down my phone started beeping. Al was asking if my work the next day was at the out-of-hours clinic held at the GP's surgery that finished at midday. By then he knew my patterns of work and where I was likely to be on certain days. I ignored him but he was right about where I would be so I fully expected him to be back on the doorstep waiting for me when I got back.

I was starting to find thoughts of Al seeping into my mind when I was concentrating at work. As I talked to patients and my colleagues, or as I sat in meetings, it was like dirty flood-water that I couldn't quite keep out with sandbags and, on that Saturday morning, a picture of Al hanging around waiting for me at home popped into my head a few times as I talked to patients and I had to snap myself back into the moment.

How will I get rid of him this time? I wondered. It felt relentless. It was like a game of cat and mouse.

I was almost certain by this point that Al would be waiting for me when I got back to the flat. I had driven into work and on the journey home I pulled into a car park and just sat and waited for an hour or so, hoping that Al would get bored, think he had got my shifts wrong and leave. The minutes seemed to tick by slowly as I tried hopelessly to listen to a drama on Radio 4. My mind switched constantly to what would be waiting for me at home. As I approached the driveway Al was there, clutching a large bouquet of bright flowers and a heart-shaped red box which was presumably chocolates. He saw me but I didn't stop and I quickly reversed back onto the street, pushed the gear stick into second and sped off. I just didn't want to talk to him. I couldn't. I had nothing left to say.

I drove aimlessly around the residential streets for about twenty minutes again, hoping that he would have left. It felt ridiculous that I couldn't even go back to my own home. *I can't live my life like this*, I thought. *I have to take back control*, so I decided to park up at home and make a run for the front door, completely ignoring Al.

As soon as I pulled in to park, Al opened the passenger door, which unfortunately was unlocked, and hauled himself into the passenger seat. He was so close I could almost feel his breath on my face and his leg was just an inch from mine. I felt completely powerless and I could see my hands shaking as I clutched the steering wheel like some sort of buoyancy aid.

'Get out of the car,' I ordered, as firmly as I could muster.

'No, I want to talk to you,' Al said.

The engine was still running and rather than stop in the driveway where no one could see us talking, I decided to drive back out onto the road and park, because at least there would be passers-by walking up and down the road to the local coffee shop. I just didn't know how I would get rid of him and my palms were starting to prickle with sweat.

'I've got tickets for Leeds Castle,' Al said. 'We had such a nice time there when we went last summer. Let's go there today and we'll be able to see some of the rooms that we didn't manage last time. We'll have a couple of hours there if we leave here now.'

'No, Al! I'm not going on dates with you. We're not in a relationship!'

'But I love you.'

'Get out of my car of I'll call the police,' I hit back. As I reached for my phone, which was sitting on the dashboard, he tried to snatch it from me. Adrenaline coursed through me and with what must have been a lightning-quick reaction, I speedily put it under my legs on the far side of him, so he couldn't grab hold of it.

We proceeded to have the same conversation and I was feeling increasingly panicky. I knew the only way I could get him out of the car was to say I would meet him and I told him he could come back to the flat on the following Monday. I told him that if he came back before then, I would call the police. I don't think he took me seriously, because I pulled away, again completing a loop of the nearby streets, and as I parked up in my space, Al popped his head out of the porch.

As he approached the car, I mouthed to him, 'I'm going to call the police.'

I hastily dialled '999', and told them what was happening.

'Please come quickly! He just won't leave me alone and I'm scared,' I said, registering the shock on Al's face that I had actually made the call.

The police car probably arrived within two or three minutes, but by then he had scarpered. The officers quickly went round the block to see if they could catch him and told me a man matching his description had been seen getting the bus.

The policemen stayed with me for a while and I gave them the history over a cup of tea. My hands were quivering and I was struggling to not cry as I gave them a summarized version of events. They agreed that the situation was spiralling out of control and told me they would come and arrest him when I had agreed to meet him. It was the best solution, they argued. He was definitely harassing me and under the Protection from Harassment Act they could issue him with a restraining order and ban him from the area. If he tried to do the same thing then, he would be arrested. I couldn't quite believe that things had got to this point but I felt hopeful that this would be enough to stop him in his tracks.

That weekend I had a constant stomach ache with the thought of double-crossing Al. I knew I had to do it, but it felt so contrived, underhand and blatant. Yet I knew I had no choice.

The following Monday evening the police called: they were all set to arrest Al. I texted Al telling him again to come to the flat and when it looked like he was running late, I phoned to ask him where he was. I was worried he would think something was up but he always answered immediately, ecstatic that I had called him.

I just wanted it over and done with. Two young and good-looking policemen pulled up outside and came in. One of them was six foot tall with blond curls and looked like he was straight out of one of those Hollywood cop shows. He told me his name was Rick. I sat on the sofa, immobilized with nerves.

When there was a knock at the door, one of the policemen went to answer it. I could hear him say, 'Al Dhalla?'

'Yes.'

'We're going to take you in for a bit of questioning.'

His voice was loud and incandescent. 'No, Alison, nooooo! She invited me to dinner! Alison, why are you doing this?'

'Come with us, please,' one of the policemen replied.

He was cautioned in the normal way. The charge at this stage was simple: Level 2 harassment.

And that was it. The door shut with a bang and I breathed a huge sigh of relief. I peered through the window and could see Al's back as he walked alongside them. *They will sort him out*, I thought. I glanced over to the porch, where there was another huge bunch of flowers – roses and tulips this time – and yet another box of chocolates. I was starting to run out of ideas about what to do with Al's gifts. I never ate any of the chocolates he gave me because by this point I had realized that it wasn't too far-fetched to imagine him poisoning them, and while the flowers were beautiful, I couldn't bear to look at them, so I ended up just dumping them in the bin.

Al was held in custody overnight and was apparently very

angry; they later told me he was banging on the door, screaming and shouting to be let out. The following day, one of the policemen called to tell me that Al had appeared in court on charges of harassment and theft of property. He had pleaded not guilty but been released on bail. The magistrates additionally placed a restraining order on him, which banned him from entering Sussex. If he came into the county, he would be arrested again. There was also a restraining order banning him from coming near me, my family and Nick.

Nothing would be left to chance.

I felt a real sense of relief that I wouldn't be finding him on my doorstep again. However, I now felt a new level of fear at the thought that I'd double-crossed Al. I had witnessed before how angry he could get, and something told me there was more to come . . .

I still felt I had to prove myself at work, but I was also certain that I could do my job and do it competently. I just wanted some sort of normality in my life, so I threw myself headlong into being the best doctor I could be. I was still on the psychiatry ward and thankfully it was a slower pace there than some of the placements I had been on. It was also a very friendly environment; the consultants would offer to take us all to the pub for a drink after a shift and, while not completely unheard of in other parts of the hospital, this kind of team-working was fairly unusual. It was a good job for me to be doing at the time because, despite the issue of the letters, I felt really supported. After all, these people were experts in mental health and bizarre behaviour.

I was still getting used to being single and being in the house on my own, and outside of work I cooked myself meals, watched TV and slept as much as possible.

Despite being banned from contacting me, Al continued to call, text and email. I remember lying in my bed at night, my phone silenced and sitting on my bedside table. It would be dark in the room, except for the odd glint of light peeking out of the curtains and silver reflections dancing across the TV screen. I would be fighting sleep but my eyes would be getting heavy and my limbs loose, then my phone would start buzzing rudely and impatiently, vibrating against the wood of the table. My eyes would dart open and my heart would start bashing against my chest as the name shone in the dark, 'Al'. He left many, many voicemails, none of which I listened to.

Two weeks later on a Monday I was at an outpatient clinic, talking to patients with alcohol addiction issues, discussing detox programmes available in the area and conducting basic medical assessments. As I was going about my work, I looked up and saw a policeman walking into the clinic; I was used to seeing uniformed men and women around because many of the patients were often in and out of prison. Coincidentally it was Rick, who had been one of the policemen who had been there when Al was arrested. I assumed he was there to talk about one of my patients on the ward and I asked him to wait in a small clinic room alongside the main ward while I finished my appointment with the lady I was with.

'Hi Alison,' he said, when I walked in, closing the door behind me. 'How are you?'

'I'm fine,' I said. 'You know, just getting on with things.'

There was then a moment's silence as I waited for the question about one of my patients.

'I've got something to tell you,' he continued. 'I don't want to worry you too much but Al has been arrested. In Wiltshire.'

It was a bit of a bolt from the blue. I couldn't quite piece together both the fact that Rick was there to see me and also the fact that Al was in Wiltshire and that he had been arrested. What on earth was he doing there? He didn't know anyone in Wiltshire. Al had told me he had a new job; what had happened to that? I knew that being out of a job and then finding himself arrested again, he had just dramatically increased the chance of him being unable to stay in the country. He was clearly on some sort of downward spiral of destruction.

Rick didn't know any of the details of the arrest but I didn't automatically assume that the news meant that I was in any danger; I still didn't think Al wished me physical harm. But I also knew that I was the person he knew the best in the UK and it's human nature to turn to the person you are closest to in times of trouble. I felt then that he would come and find me regardless of where he was now or what had happened.

Rick told me that one of the more senior detectives would come and talk to me about safety precautions, and minutes later an older lady came into the room we were in and asked me some questions about Al and how he might be feeling. She also took my photo. The whole experience was very surreal.

'We don't want to scare you,' she said. 'But we want to monitor your safety. I would like to tag your phone and put your house on red alert, so if you phone the police will come immediately.'

She also asked how I was feeling; had I ever considered suicide? I think I actually laughed. I wasn't feeling that way. I was shocked, yes, but still too naive about the risk I was potentially under. This was the question I asked patients every day; I didn't expect her to then ask me the same thing. But at that time stalking wasn't considered a crime and was often put in the same bracket as domestic abuse, so I guess many women she saw had been worn down by their partners to breaking point by the time the police became involved.

She asked for the addresses of my different workplaces, including the psychiatric hospital, the drug addiction unit and the ward in the hospital where I was expecting to start my placement in obstetrics and gynaecology the next day. She also enquired about how I felt about going home to my flat and whether I could manage by myself. I insisted I wanted to stay, so she told me that she would text morning and evening to check in on me and make sure that I was OK.

'Is there anyone you could stay with?' she asked.

I considered this for a moment. None of my friends knew the full extent of what was happening and I didn't want to pull someone else into what was already a very complicated situation. My family had already taken enough hits because of my relationship with Al; the last thing I wanted to do was pull someone else into the picture. I knew the best thing would be to stay at the flat and try to get on with my life. Also

I didn't feel that scared. I never thought he would hurt me physically; this was the man who claimed I was the love of his life. Ironically, I was more concerned for him.

That day when I left work, leaving the safe confines of the hospital walls behind me, I slowly started to feel more self-conscious. I had no idea whether Al was still in custody and I was certain that, if he was released, he would come back to me like a homing pigeon or hunting animal. I considered walking first, then I debated getting the bus, or even a taxi. Would I be safe? Was Al going to hurt me? The idea started to trickle into my mind and sat there.

I decided to catch the bus and as I found a seat and we bumped along down the road, slowly but surely I started feeling more and more scared. My senses were heightened; every noise was magnified and every move I made felt slow and deliberate. I scanned every face to see if I could see Al; I surveyed for dark skin, brooding eyes, desperate looks. As we pulled up to the stop nearest my flat I examined the dirty pavements, the people waiting at the stop – teens, old people with walking sticks, other professionals – then took in the wider picture, my eyes scanning like a camera panning out.

I raced round the corner towards my flat with my head and shoulders hunched. When I was through the door, I bolted through the rooms, looking in cupboards and under the bed, like a child scared of monsters. Once I had reassured myself Al wasn't there, I locked the door behind me. In fact, at that point Sussex police were trying to get Wiltshire to hold him, but there was still a chance that he could be released after twenty-four hours. In the end they managed to hold him for a further twelve hours because they were concerned he was some sort of terrorist, or posed a dangerous threat.

Mum and David, who were on holiday on the island of Lundy, just off the Devon coastline, had also been informed by the Thames Valley Police of the turn of events. The trip to the remote isle was something they had planned since the start of 2010 to mark David's retirement in 2011, and it was something they had been meaning to do for a while before that. Later that night Mum left me a voicemail. She didn't have any reception but had called from the payphone in the hotel where she was staying and left a message for me. I was at home in my flat when I dialled my voicemail with shaky fingers.

'Hi darling, I do hope you're OK. I'm calling from the payphone because we don't have any reception out here. I'm not sure what you've been told but we've been informed that Al was arrested with a weapon in Wiltshire. A crossbow, the police said. Please look after yourself, sweetheart. We've been told to be cautious and that if Al is released, plans will be made to ensure our safety. Please let me know how you are if you can or I'll call you again as soon as I can.'

For a long time I sat on the floor stunned and horrified. A million thoughts went through my head: why had he purchased a weapon like that. Did this man actually want to kill me? Kill my parents? Kill one of us? It seemed so surreal, so barbaric and so unlike the Al that I had known. What the hell was he up to? I felt scared in a way I had never felt before. I feared for my life.

*

That night I slept under the table in my living room wearing my clothes and trainers in case I needed to get up and run. I was convinced I would never be able to sleep but in the end I dropped off in the early hours. When I did eventually sleep, I dreamt like a drunk person, a kaleidoscope of vivid, bright images colliding into each other.

The floor felt hard and uncomfortable, and my body ached all over, but I knew I needed to get up and go through the motions.

Get dressed, breakfast, work.

I pulled myself up off the floor and after a quick wash I threw on my default outfit: black work trousers and a smart top. On top of everything else going on, I had an induction for a new job that morning, in obstetrics and gynaecology. I didn't know how I would concentrate through the thick fog in my head. I made myself a cup of tea; even that small task seemed to take more brainpower than I could manage. I put the mug to my lips and drank it quickly, gulping without tasting, and it scalded my tongue.

I automatically opened the cupboard doors but didn't want breakfast; just the thought of food made me feel nauseous. My stomach churned angrily and noisily. Since Al's arrest, I'd found myself grabbing food at work and trying to eat it quickly without thinking. I felt constantly sick. I couldn't concentrate on anything and the idea of going to a super-market and actually cooking something seemed too hard. Like running a marathon. Even though it had only been less than twenty-four hours, the flat was becoming messy with clothes strewn around and the washing machine rammed with dirty clothes; I just couldn't face doing anything.

I carefully looked out the window to see if there was any movement in the bushes or at the end of the road. I only had to walk around the corner to the hospital lecture theatre for the induction, probably no more than a one or two-minute walk, but it seemed so dangerous. I put on my trainers, reasoning that they would be most comfortable if I had to run fast. In my clammy, damp hand I clutched my phone. The emergency dial would take just one touch.

I bolted and slammed the door behind me without looking back and walked fast, almost running. My head spun around constantly. The road, the trees, driveways, bushes, parked cars, moving cars . . . everything seemed like a potential threat.

As I rounded the corner of my street onto the main road I felt a little safer and my breathing slowed slightly; there were more people milling around, also starting their days. They would help me if Al approached and I started screaming, wouldn't they?

Reaching the hospital, I quickly went inside the doors to the education block and to the warmth of the musty lecture theatre and immediately I felt more secure and cushioned from the outside. I was surrounded by good friends and work colleagues – medical people who were kind and reliable. Inside I would be safe; it was outside when he was going to get me. The fear was slowly replaced by a deep numbness. I took my seat, got out my pen and paper and listened as best I could to what I could expect over the coming weeks.

The morning passed in a bit of a blur and I tried desperately to switch off all my thoughts of Al. It was almost impossible but for brief moments I managed it as I tried to grapple with some new medical fact or detail of the placement.

That afternoon I was due to be working in the Princess Royal Hospital at Haywards Heath, where I would be on call that weekend. The facility was attached to the larger teaching hospital in Brighton, and as part of my learning I would be doing a stint at the maternity unit there. Fortunately one of my work colleagues, a guy by the name of Ben, who had some idea of what was happening in my personal life, offered to drive me over there and take me home later that day.

The police were leaving me voicemails and keeping me abreast of what was going on. While I had known he was behind bars the night before, I had a hunch that the evidence wouldn't be strong enough to keep him there and my fear was justified. I learned that, in spite of Sussex's protestations, Al had been released after coming before the magistrate in Wiltshire. Although he had clearly breached his bail conditions imposed by Sussex, he could only be tried in Wiltshire for the crimes committed in Wiltshire, which was driving without a valid license. Whether or not the magistrate was made aware of the wider story, I don't know. Al had pleaded guilty, been given a fine and bailed. He was back on the loose.

On our return to the flat I remember thanking Ben, looking around, scanning the road again and then running from his car into my home, with my head down. I was paranoid that Al might see me with another guy and his suspicions might be aroused and he would have another reason to be angry. Meanwhile I was keen to keep the pretence of vague normality up in front of Ben, which was hard.

I stood on the doorstep, fumbling with my keys, the cold metal slipping through my fingers. I wished I could move quicker but I seemed paralysed and clumsy. Finally the key was in and I twisted the lock, ran inside and slammed the door hard behind me. A quick look around my flat revealed there was no one inside. The bathroom, kitchen, under the bed and table were all clear. He wasn't hiding in the cupboards waiting to leap out and get me. Sometimes I thought I was being ridiculous, but other times I thought maybe this was my new normal, maybe this was just the way I would have to live.

I couldn't do anything that night. I had the following day off so there would be nothing to distract myself then either, nowhere to escape from my dark thoughts. I wondered what to do. I made a cup of tea and hid in the kitchen, trying to decide how to pass the time that evening and whether to keep the curtains open so that I could see if he came near, or close them, so that he couldn't see me. I kept the lights off and decided to keep the curtains open. I needed to know if he was approaching. I sat in the corner so that I had a good view out of all the windows, looking so hard my eyes started to glaze over. I was marking time and waiting for something to happen; I knew it was going to happen, I just wasn't sure when or where. I was terrified but, equally, I couldn't bear living my life like that anymore, and I knew the situation needed to end. I was still struggling to reconcile the person found with a crossbow with the Al I knew. He wouldn't hurt me, would he? He claimed to love and adore me.

Eventually I decided I needed to have a wash and get ready for bed. I checked in with the police from my phone and told them I was fine, but I didn't want to move from my watch post. I finally decided to have a quick shower – the quickest shower I've ever had. It must've lasted all of about ten seconds. I couldn't have him finding me with no clothes on, dragging me outside, and me having to flee for my life, naked.

I pulled on my jogging bottoms and a sweatshirt, socks and trainers. I needed to sleep in clothes because I didn't want to make a run for it in pyjamas. I needed to be prepared.

Dusk came and eventually I decided to close the curtains and use the light from my phone to move around, and I made my bed again under the table. This second night I was so tired, but I lay there fully clothed, alert and waiting. My trainers felt so uncomfortable on my feet, so eventually I kicked them off and finally drifted off to sleep.

In the early hours I was awoken by deep voices.

'This is the police. This is the police. Open up.' A bright yellow torchlight shone through the curtains from side to side, illuminating the inky darkness of the flat. My hand was still grasping my phone ready to dial '999'. I couldn't be sure it was them. At that point, I didn't trust a soul. I peered through the curtains; there were three men in uniform. They looked like the police.

I went to the door and opened it cautiously, peering out through a small crack.

'Alison Hewitt?'

'Yes,' I replied. I breathed a sigh of relief – it was the police. Whatever I'd been waiting for, it had finally had happened. My heart was pounding but I found this weird sense of release wash over me: had they caught him? What had he done? Had they got to him before he got to me?

I stepped back, glad of my joggers. It was Rick again. I was happy to see a friendly face.

'We've got some information,' he said, a grim look on his face. I held my breath. A lump lodged itself in my throat.

'Someone has set fire to your mum's house.'

'What?' I gasped. This wasn't what I had imagined. My stomach lurched into my mouth. Mum and David were away, so my first thought was relief that they were safe. It didn't occur to me that the house was attached to the neighbour's cottage and they were asleep next door.

'We don't have any more information than that,' he continued.

'Shit,' I said. 'It's thatched! If it reaches the roof, the whole thing could go up!' I felt a pang for the beautiful old cottage where I had grown up.

'You need to pack a bag and come to the police station. You can't stay here. We are waiting on more information. As soon as I find out anything, I'll let you know.'

It must be Al, I thought. I knew it was, but I could hardly believe it. *How could he do something like this?*

I had no idea what to take with me – I knew there was a possibility that he would set fire to my flat too. I rushed to the bathroom, splashed cold water on my face, put a brush through my knotted hair. Then I found a change of clothing, clean underwear and deodorant. I looked around, and picked up my wallet and phone. Nothing else seemed that important. We were just about to leave when I turned back and caught sight of my pink filing box, which contained my renewed passport, insurance, birth certificate and bank details.

'Can I just get my pink file too?' I asked.

'If you need to, but just take the minimum. You can come back and collect some more stuff later with someone.'

I picked up the pink file and I'm glad I did – later it was considered too dangerous for me to return.

I left the flat and stepped into the back of the police car. I noted that another police car was sitting outside my flat as surveillance.

At the station, I was taken to an interrogation room while I waited for a detective to come.

'Here's your tea,' he said. 'I'll try and find out what is happening. I will report back as soon as I can.'

I was on my own and quickly went from feeling full of adrenaline, to suddenly tired and very, very drained, almost as if I could sleep there and then. I finally felt safe and as if I didn't need to be constantly on my guard. My eyelids felt heavy and my limbs like lead.

The detective returned and told me he had no more information and that I would need to be questioned later. We made small talk and I told him about the job I was supposed to be starting, saying thankfully that day, which was a Friday, was my day off because I was due to be on call that weekend. My work wouldn't be disturbed. That seemed to be of paramount importance at that time. The one bit of normality that I clung to, like a float adrift at sea.

His radio suddenly beeped and I heard tinny shouting. It was nothing to do with me: there were reports of a man exposing himself to some people along the seafront – a very different job to attend to, I thought to myself.

My stomach gurgled and I needed the loo. I went to find it and while I was there I felt freaked out all over again. That feeling of terror just crept up on me from nowhere. The light seemed to glance off the tiles; was he in there? Was he hiding? My heart started ramming against my chest like it might burst out. I quickly retreated back to the interrogation room. I rested my head on the table. I was so weary, it was as if a fraying thread was holding my limbs together.

The detective wanted to know where all my family were: I told him Mum and my stepdad were on Lundy Island and that my brother Paul was in Buckinghamshire, but when they asked for an address, I was stumped. I didn't have an address for him. I told them he was living on a canal boat last time we talked and that I knew he sometimes stayed at a friend's caravan that was parked in woods somewhere.

The policeman seemed happy. They had been talking to Thames Valley police and decided that if we didn't know where Paul was then it was unlikely that Al would be able to locate him either. I was relieved; clearly there were some benefits to his alternative lifestyle. But I was still worried about him and wanted to speak to him. He was a bit hit-and-miss with communication and although he now had a mobile phone, it was most often turned off, or not charged.

'I really want to talk to him,' I told the policeman. I felt desperate to hear his voice.

'Yes. If you get hold of him, tell him to report to the nearest police station.' They now knew the threat wasn't just towards me but my whole family and were eager for us all to be in police care.

They gave me a phone and I punched his number into it but there was no answer. I willed him to pick up. I tried again but just got his voicemail.

'Hi, this is Paul. Sorry I'm not here to take your call. Leave a message after the beep.' I told him to call me as soon as he got the message.

I hoped he was still asleep. Five minutes later I still desperately wanted to speak to him so I tried again. I needed to talk to him.

Eventually, he picked up, his voice bleary with sleep and confusion.

'Hello?'

Relief washed through me. At least I knew he was OK. It also felt good to hear a familiar voice. It was the best sound I had heard for days.

'Paul, it's me. Alison. Something's happened.'

I knew he could hear the panic in my voice. It was only 5.30 a.m.

His voice became much clearer then. 'What?' He was alarmed too.

I told him Mum's house had been set on fire and repeated what I knew, which wasn't much, and the fact I was at the police station.

He sounded shaken but not overly worried about his own safety. He told me he was staying at the friend's caravan in the middle of a forest I'd never heard of and I told him to go to the nearest police station. I was paranoid that Al would find him.

'He'll never find me here in Milton Keynes,' he said.

'I need you to go and do what they say,' I pleaded with him. He agreed and said he would get someone to drive him there and would call me once he had arrived.

The time ticked slowly by and at some point I must have nodded off . . .

I awoke to the sight of another policeman dressed in a grey suit. I felt unembarrassed that I had been asleep on the table in the waiting room but my neck felt stiff. He put out his hand and introduced himself as Colin. He was tall with piercing blue eyes. He told me he was from the anti-victimization unit.

'Bring your stuff upstairs,' he said. 'I'm afraid we'll need more statements. We'll have a briefing first thing in the morning and I'll know more then.'

I followed him, trudging up some stairs, and sat at a small, empty work station. I looked around me and there on the wall was my photo, about a passport picture size, listed under 'vulnerable women in the city' along with nine another women.

I couldn't get over it. I didn't feel like I was similar to any of these women; I would never have thought of myself as vulnerable before that point. The faces on the wall were of women whose partners came to see me in the psychiatric unit, who had a history of violence; of women who might be beaten up or worse. The drug addicts, whose partners were in and out of prison, who I talked to and had meetings about with senior staff in order to find the best route to getting them clean. There I was pinned next to these people, in this little row of faces who were in danger. Clearly I was as much at risk as them.

I sat there appalled. I felt very in the dark but safe for the first time in so long. I believed they were doing their job.

I continued to wait and was told Mum and David were being airlifted out of Lundy by helicopter and we would be reunited before long. I wondered how Mum would feel about the house. I felt so sorry and sad about everything I had put them through.

As the time ticked past, more information about his arrest in Wiltshire began to trickle out. The day before Rick came to see me at the hospital, Al had been arrested in a field in the middle of Wiltshire firing a crossbow. He had mounted targets on straw bales on a farmer's land. Wiltshire Police had sent an armed response unit to the scene and he was arrested. When the police asked what he was doing he replied that he was 'just out for a drive and doing what all young Canadian men do – shooting in the countryside.' The policeman who arrested him later admitted that Al seemed to 'stare through him', making him feel so uncomfortable that he kept his palm touching his handgun throughout the exchange in case he needed to use it.

Al was driving a white van at the time and was evasive about where he had bought it from, saying he had purchased it from 'somewhere near Putney'. When asked for his documentation, he showed the police a Canadian ID and a driving licence which had expired in December 2010. The police could not verify if he had insurance and although you can drive on a foreign driving licence in the UK for up to a year he was arrested for licence and insurance infringements and charged with trespass with a firearm.

In the van they had found an air rifle, with telescopic sight, silencer and pellets, a BB gun and a handheld crossbow and bolts. They checked the air rifle but discovered that the performance of the air rifle was just below the level at which a licence is required. Al was charged with possession of a weapon capable of wounding, trespass with a firearm and driving licence and insurance offences.

The true extent of what they found in his van wasn't revealed at the time and it was only when we eventually ended up in court that I found out how sinister the set-up was. I think the police told us what they felt was appropriate for us to know at the time. During the court case we discovered that not only had the grill behind the front seats, which normally protects the driver and the front passengers from materials stacked in the back, been removed, but the rear window had also been taken out. The police reasoned that this would allow him to move from the driver's seat to the rear of the van without getting out and he would be able to fire a weapon through the rear window without being observed. Added to this, there were some pretty strange contents inside. They found a map of the Princess Royal Hospital at Haywards Heath where I was due to start placement at the maternity unit the next day, and in the van they found black refuse bags and a toolbox containing a hammer, goggles, scissors, superglue, a knife, Allen keys, a gas torch, a claw hammer and plastic gloves.

In the favourites on Al's satnav were many addresses that related to my life and also stored was the location of Luckwell Bridge in Exmoor, which is on the road to Ilfracombe where the boat to Lundy sails from. Everything pointed to Al planning a revenge attack. He was clearly intent on getting me back anyway he could and settling whatever score he had in his mind with Mum. He may have been planning to meet them off the ferry or even sail across to Lundy himself.

Back at the police station, the questions about Al started: who did he bank with? I couldn't remember. I must have seen him withdraw money from cashpoints hundreds of times but clearly it didn't register. Then I was asked about his job: who was he working for? I wasn't sure as I purposely hadn't engaged him in talk about his new life in London. I wanted him to get on with it and find happiness away from me.

I was then asked my story and for details of text messages from him – which I had deleted one morning, while I was sitting in a small cafe in Hove not long after my return from Thailand, in a futile bid to detox him from my life. I painstakingly highlighted every last one of them, pressed delete and watched them vanish from my screen. For a few hours I had felt so much better and I thought I might be able to put him behind me and move on with my life, but in hindsight it was a stupid thing to do because it was valuable evidence that could have been used against him. Fortunately I kept all my missed call history and all the emails he had sent me over the previous few months.

I logged in to my email account and opened the file where I had put everything for the police, under previous instructions from my liaison officer, Emily.

'Oh my goodness,' Colin said as he started to scroll down the hundreds and hundreds of emails. *It's going to take him a long, long time to read all those*, I thought. I know he was looking for something threatening but there was nothing in there that said he was out to get me physically. I was still struggling to reconcile the guy who I knew, who had never once threatened my physically or sexually, with the man I was quickly learning was far, far more dangerous than I could ever have previously imagined.

Emily then came in. She had previously helped me organize some of my evidence such as cards, letters, flowers and chocolates that Al had given me, which I had then dropped into the police station for their records. She told me she would help me write my statement. I knew it was going to take a long time and people kept coming in asking questions about Al: how tall was he? What was the exact colour of his eyes? What was he wearing the last time I saw him? I did my best to answer them, but felt so inadequate. Why didn't I take more notice of the small things?

Emily told me that the police had put out red alerts on all my workplaces and that they had even gone in and given talks to some consultants and security staff at the psychiatric hospital. When one of my doctor friends texted asking if I was alright and if there was anything she could do to help, I knew then that the drama I had been so keen to hide from my workmates was probably spreading its way along the hospital grapevine.

The police also alerted the security staff at the Princess Royal Hospital in Haywards Heath and told them I wouldn't be in for my shift the next day in the maternity unit. I found this really unsettling. I wasn't even a day into this new job and already something had gone wrong. It wasn't what I wanted after the turmoil of the inquest and then the poison pen letters ruining the last two work placements.

While I had dropped off many of the personal letters and things Al had given me to Emily, we had never gone through everything properly and made a statement, so she started to compile a detailed account of the relationship, the stalking and the letters, emails and texts. I filled her in on the ugly scene on Christmas Day where I noticed that my belongings had gone missing and were in the bin. One thing I had in my pink box which I was able to show her was a will that Al had made. I had never opened it because it was during the time I was trying to split up with him and I simply told him I wasn't interested in it. I was able to give her that and it had details of his bank account, his address in Canada and other information I think they probably found useful.

The day dragged on and, during one toilet break, I caught sight of myself in the mirror and barely recognized the woman staring back at me. My skin looked grey and mottled,

I had dark rings under my red-rimmed eyes. My stomach felt painfully empty but at the same time I knew I couldn't eat anything because of the terror churning inside me. I held on to the side of the sink to support myself; I felt like my legs were made of jelly, almost as if I were floating above the ground.

Come on, Alison, I told myself. *You've got to pull yourself together.*

I splashed my face with some water, patted it with a paper towel and walked back into the corridor, ready for the next onslaught of questions.

Every now and again Emily would report back and tell me that the police had thought they had had a sighting and it turned out that it was another Asian doctor on one of the hospital sites and not him. They clearly fully expected him to home in on one of my workplaces.

At lunchtime I went out with one of the detectives to a sandwich bar directly opposite. I didn't feel hungry but she told me that I should eat to keep my strength up. I crossed the road as quickly as I could; I felt terrified. I was convinced that Al would be able to see me and was hiding in the bushes somewhere. It took me a good half an hour after sitting back down in the police station to recover.

At some point in the late afternoon, I phoned Paul again and he told me that he was on his way to Brighton with Linus. I couldn't wait to see Paul and hug him. I was told we needed to find somewhere safe for us all, and Linus of course, in an area that Al wouldn't think we would go. There was a safe house that the police used regularly but we decided we needed to find somewhere that would take dogs and located a hotel in Eastbourne, just east of Brighton, as I had never been there with Al before. It was expensive but I didn't care; I figured that if I was going to be holed up there for a number of days then the more luxurious the better.

I continued with my statement. I knew there was a car parked outside my house on the lookout for anything suspicious, but I still felt happier at the police station. Yet as the night fell, the lights were on in the station and I knew that I could be clearly seen from the outside. I suddenly became very paranoid again and asked Emily to shut the blinds. I immediately felt better as she drew them together and we continued with the statement hidden from the outside world. Whenever I left the room to go to the toilet I ran past the windows or bent down with my hood up, even though I was high up in the building. I thought that he could easily have a gun pointing at me from somewhere.

Paul arrived and, as he pulled up, a policeman went outside and told him to park his car in the main parking area. I was so worried for him. It was so obvious it was him because of Linus, who was such as distinctive-looking dog. If Al were watching the building, he would stick out like sore thumb.

As he came in, I rushed to him and threw my arms around his solid neck. I felt myself sobbing uncontrollably as he hugged me and stroked my back. I was shocked by the intensity of how I felt and how relieved I was to see him.

'He never would have found me up there, sis,' he said.

'I know but I need you here.'

'I'm here now. It's going to be OK.'

Linus was given some water to drink while I sat gripping Paul's hand. I felt better, so much better now he had arrived. But Paul didn't want to be sitting there waiting, doing nothing; he seemed agitated and desperate to sort the situation out himself. Some friends had driven past the house in Aston Abbotts and noted that it was all taped up because of the damage he had wrought. Paul wanted to stay in Aston Abbotts and wait to see if Al returned to the house, but we all knew that this was a terrible idea.

By then it was late and I was told to surrender my ID, phone and credit card to storage before we went to the hotel in Eastbourne. One of the police had been there and said it was very old-fashioned, the sort of place where a bunch of old people would rock up at on a coach tour and complain about the lack of china. It was perfect for what we wanted. We were told not to use debit or credit cards, or any ID that could identify us. We had been booked in under different names and would stay there until they caught him.

Just before we left the station, I was told more devastating news: Al had been on the Haywards Heath hospital grounds in the early hours of the morning. Firstly, he was seen wandering around the car park in a woolly hat and gloves at 3 a.m. The security guards had asked him what he was doing as he was acting suspiciously, but they didn't know at that point that he was wanted by the police. Apparently he said he couldn't sleep but he appeared agitated and made them feel very uneasy.

But it got worse: just an hour earlier, after his picture was circulated around the hospital, he was spotted there again, this time dressed as a doctor on the ward, asking about me and my work rota.

I couldn't believe it. The news floored me. I felt my palms prickle and the tiredness I had felt earlier vanished instantly. It showed just how determined he was to get to me. Just as I was told one thing that I could never have predicted – that he'd set fire to my mum's house – I was told he had dressed as a doctor with a white coat and stethoscope slung round his neck, all so he could get to me. The whole situation seemed so unreal.

The police said that they didn't know where he was, but that he must still be close by. They were determined to catch him before he could cause any harm. He was very, very clever so they needed to outwit him.

'Is he reading your emails?' Emily asked. I was never totally sure that he was, even though the people around me were convinced that was the case. She told me that using email was our best bet to create a trap for him so I began to name some examples of things that he would only be able to find out if he was looking at my computer, such as the fact Mum and David had gone on holiday to Lundy Island.

The police had been hatching a detailed plan and Emily told me what it was.

'Right. It's obvious he has been hacking into your emails,' she told me. 'Send an email to your mum telling her you are fine and that you are finished with the police. Say you are going to work tomorrow as normal, for 8 a.m. when your shift starts.'

Slowly I started typing.

Hi Mum,
I hope you are well. I've finished with the police now. I'm
back on duty at the Princess Royal tomorrow at 8 a.m.
Speak on your return.
Love Alison

As I pressed send, Emily turned to me and squeezed my hand. 'We're going to get him, Alison,' she said. 'We're going to put him away and you won't have to be scared ever again.

Eleven

The Trap

Al had clearly been plotting while he had been behind lock and key in Wiltshire. On his release, he hired a car and drove the ninety-two miles north to Aston Abbotts, deep in thought and intent on revenge. Later that evening he had parked on one of the roads near my mum's house. Presumably too focused on his plan to notice, Al pulled up across the driveway of a retired farm manager called Brian, meaning that he blocked his car in. Thinking it strange and unusual for such a small village where people were considerate of other people's parking and so forth, Brian noted down the number plate.

In the early hours of the morning Al lit a Yellow Pages phonebook with accelerant by the side door, dropped it there and then doused diesel along the front and side of the house. It immediately caught and spread up the ancient ivy that snaked up the front of the cottage, and it was nearly at the thatch by the time Mum's neighbours Christine and Michael, who had been woken up by the smell of smoke, raced round to see what was happening. They were terrified that Mum and David were inside because their cars were still parked on the pebble driveway, and they were bashing on the door, shouting at them to wake up. Christine and Michael immediately called the fire brigade and thought it was arson because of the nature of the bright yellow, orange and red flames that were spreading in a uniform fashion along the front and side of the house, blocking both exits. If the thatch had gone up in a fireball, then the whole house would have been destroyed, along with next door, where the neighbour was sound asleep in the upstairs bedroom. He was in grave danger that night. We will never know if Al targeted the two doors to block Mum and David's exit – that's something we can only speculate about – but it was a clear sign of Al's state of mind.

It was two to three hours later when Al was spotted in the car park of the Princess Royal Hospital wearing black woolly gloves and a beanie hat. A security guard having a sneaky cigarette spotted him at about 3 a.m., and after being challenged by him and a couple of his colleagues, Al insisted he was walking around the car park simply because he couldn't sleep. The security staff didn't know Al was wanted, so he was free to plot his next move.

That day he transferred all his money back to Canada and it was clear that he was working towards some sort of end game. The police later said that the state he was in suggested that he expected to go to prison forever, or even to die. He no longer cared about anything else except exacting payback.

After the arson attack and with all my workplaces on red alert, the police circulated his picture to the staff at the hospital and one of the midwives said that they had seen him dressed as a doctor with a white coat, a stethoscope around his neck and a folder under his arm that day. She had presumed he was one of the new batch of doctors, who were due to start the next day – of which I, of course, was one. Al had been buzzed into the ward, which should have been only accessible to a member of the public using a special electronic access code by a 'newly delivered' father. One of the midwives on duty said she was surprised to see him wearing a white coat, because most doctors these days didn't wear one, and that she thought it was strange that he was enquiring about the rota. Apparently he mentioned that Dr Eli was responsible for coordinating it – a clear sign he was accessing all my emails, as how else could he have known?

She told him they were busy and to come back the next day but he returned just fifteen minutes later and was seen speaking to one of the junior doctors, who said he didn't have the rota on him but gave Al his email address and said he would see him at the induction the following day. One of the onlookers noted that Al didn't seem to be looking at the junior doctor in the eye as they talked but instead seemed more interested on the noticeboard over his shoulder. Later, the midwives who had witnessed the exchange discussed it because it seemed so unusual and noted his lack of hospital ID, usually on a lanyard around the necks of all the staff there. The midwife checked with security, who showed her stills of the man who had been acting suspiciously the previous night. The security guard confirmed that it was the same person and that Al was wanted by the police. But it was too late to get him then – Al was already on the road again.

We'll never know his exact movements but thanks to CCTV footage we know that he did later return to the scene of the fire at Aston Abbotts, as Paul had predicted he might. This is a common theme with many arsonists, who go back to watch the fire burn and revel in the devastation they have caused. However, Al saw that the place was surrounded by police with hi-vis jackets but also more importantly that it was still standing and, in a rage, he drove off to Wing. There he tried to set fire to the unmanned police station using an old *Evening Standard* newspaper, which failed to catch and cause any damage to any of the brickwork but charred all the bushes next to the building. A policeman, on his return from being called out, was only alerted to it when he smelt the strong odour of petrol and discovered dark patches around the building where the liquid had been poured.

The police knew they weren't far behind him. I prayed that the email sting would work but I wasn't holding my breath – he kept outwitting all of us and seemed to be always one step ahead, wrong-footing the police at every turn.

That night, after hours of questioning, an undercover police car drove Paul, Linus and me from the station to the 'safe house' hotel in Eastbourne with another car tailing us. Nothing was being left to chance. Paul, Linus and I were squashed in the back seat and there were two policemen in the front but I was still paranoid and terrified. I had my hood up and head down and shouted at Paul for not wearing a hat; I was convinced that Al would recognize us. It was pitch black outside but I was certain he would be lurking somewhere and see Linus and then realize that Paul was with me. I was physically shaking all over; my hands trembled and every hair on my body seemed to stand on end. My heart banged in my chest and it echoed noisily in my head, my ears, my neck and my tummy. I kept thinking about if I would be able to hurt another human being in order to protect myself. Would I really be able to stand there with a kitchen knife or another heavy household item and actually use it until help arrived? Would I find it in myself to injure another person? I didn't know if I could.

Then 'what ifs' started to pile up in my brain: what if Al had shot someone with a weapon? What if Mum and David had been in the house when it went up in flames? What if the neighbour had been harmed in the fire? What if Al had really succeeded in whatever he had set out to do? If I actually lived to see what happened, would I ever be able to live with myself? Thoughts were racing so fast through my head I thought I might pass out.

When we pulled up outside the hotel, the police assured us that there would be a car sitting outside all night, with police checking the area. Even so, I felt manic with fear as I ran inside, unashamed by my reaction. I was sharing a twin room with Paul and Linus, which made me feel a little bit safer. Up until that point I felt I had dealt with what had happened largely on my own but at least now I was with someone else, and if Al came to get me there would be another person in the room. I immediately drew the heavy brown curtains together because the room overlooked the grounds of the hotel and checked the bathroom, scanning the bath, inside the cupboards and under the bed. I looked in every nook and cranny, where it would be impossible for a human to hide but I needed to satisfy myself that we were alone and he wasn't there, waiting. When I went to the loo I deliberately wouldn't shut the bathroom door and didn't care that Paul was sitting outside on the bed, stroking Linus's silky head. I needed to see another human. I couldn't bear to be on my own.

At 11.30 p.m. that night we were reunited with Mum and David. I sprinted down the anonymous corridor to their room, feeling a mixture of terror at the situation and relief that they had arrived and were safe, but found that their reaction was a different one to mine. They were full of stories about the drama of being lifted off Lundy at 5 o'clock in the morning where they had been met at the helicopter with two policemen wearing black balaclavas carrying guns. They couldn't get over how surreal the experience was and laughed as they said they felt like extras in a film. Mum, who was in all of a fluster, kept saying that she had forgotten to pack her knickers and David was worried because on Lundy no one used money and simply settled their tabs with the hotels, bars and shops on leaving. They had been whisked away so quickly he hadn't been able to pay their tabs and was mortified. I think, for them, the fact that we were safe and the damage to the house was superficial was almost good news because it could have been so, so much worse. I know they were scared too but I was paralysed with fear. A deep feeling of dread had lodged itself through me, like an iron stake. I couldn't laugh or be happy or even engage with the conversation. Part of me also felt horribly guilty. I knew that ultimately it was my choices that were somewhat to blame for everything that had happened.

Much of that evening is a blur, as if I was looking in on myself. My head felt thick with noise, panic and thoughts. Back in our room, we settled down for the night. Paul dropped off quickly, snoring softly in the bed beside mine, Linus curled regally at his feet, with his head on his paw. I spent much of the night lying on the floor, against the worn brown carpet, looking at the light under the door. I knew if I could see the dark shadow of footsteps approaching, I would be ready to run, call the police or fight for my life. My skin crawled with adrenaline, my breath was ragged and I had constant pins and needles. But I knew that any attempt to sleep that night would be futile. He could appear at any minute. I had to be prepared.

Al rose to the bait.

The phone in our room at the hotel started ringing shortly after 7 a.m. I must've dropped off just before dawn but I immediately jumped up off the floor to pick it up, knowing instinctively it was the police with news. Al had surprised them by turning up an hour earlier than expected at the Princess Royal Hospital. Staff had seen him on the grounds and raised the alarm. They had recognized him from a still image from the hospital's CCTV that had been circulated the previous day. An early morning planning meeting at the police station had been interrupted and cars hurriedly dispatched to their intercept points.

I relayed the message to Paul and we sat on the end of our beds in silence, willing the phone to ring again. The wait was painfully slow and the seconds seemed to tick past laboriously, like dripping molasses. I had my head in my hands, muttering to myself.

At 7.30 a.m. the phone rang again. They'd caught him.

Al had finally been captured in a toilet at the hospital. He was hiding in there having got wind of the fact he had been clocked by the staff, again wearing his props: a white coat and stethoscope. Staff had been told to avoid him at all costs but with great presence of mind the nurses who had seen him pushed a large laundry cage up against the loo door blocking his exit. Two teams of armed police had entered the loos and tried to arrest him, telling him to put his hands on his head, but he didn't comply and struggled to escape. They were able to grab him but it was difficult to get handcuffs on him and restrain him.

After searching the grounds, they found another car he had hired. My hunch that he would easily and quickly be able to get hold of the same equipment he had been found with in Wiltshire had been correct: in the boot were many of the same things he had stored in the white van, which had been impounded after his arrest in Wiltshire. It contained a high-powered, loaded crossbow and a knife. On the satnav of this car was a secluded area in woodland near the hospital. Clearly he intended to get me out of the hospital and to this site.

When I heard the news I couldn't stop shaking. I felt so

many things at once: relief, joy, apprehension, fear and giddiness. It was the most bizarre feeling and I just lay on the bed, trying to get my head around it all.

Hanging up the receiver, I told Paul, 'They've got him. They arrested him in the hospital toilets.'

Paul started whooping with excitement and rushed through to share the news with Mum and David, who started dancing around their room. They rushed back and we all hugged each other joyfully. I don't think it really hit me that they had finally got him but I was definitely happy; the weight of the threat against me was finally starting to lift.

We decided to go down to breakfast and, having not eaten anything proper for a few days, I suddenly felt ravenous. As we entered the dining room, all around us were well-heeled and refined elderly men and women tucking into their breakfasts with polished silver cutlery, while we must've looked a right state. There was a clear 'no jeans and trainers' rule at the hotel but because we had all rushed there in such a panic, we were all in blue tatty jeans, creased T-shirts and muddy trainers. Around us the conversation seemed to revolve around the grapefruit not being properly segmented and the toast being a 'trifle dark'. It was completely bizarre because it was so irrelevant.

We spent most of that day at Eastbourne police station. Mum, David and I were each closeted in separate rooms with different policemen, who helped us to fill out our statement forms on computers. The factual part was relatively easy except that the chronological order of things was already beginning to get confused in my head. It felt like a year's worth of events had happened in a few days, like the storyline to some sort of gritty soap opera. When it came to the personal statement at the end about how the experience had affected me, I needed help. I found myself very tearful and struggled to swallow; it was as if there was a large golf ball wedged in my throat. Emily was kind and let me take my time, helping me put my feelings into words.

Later in the evening we decided to go into Eastbourne. As we walked along the beach and watched the waves crash against the shore, I realized it was over. The police had said he would almost certainly remain in custody until the case went to court. We knew we were safe for the time being. Paul had spent the day exploring with Linus and had found a rustic pub for us to have dinner in, just up the road in Beachy Head. We ordered and sat out in the evening sun. David had developed a cold and a hacking cough. During a particularly nasty bout of coughing, I said in my unemotional doctor's tone, 'The trouble is that coughs are exasperated by stress,' and we all fell about laughing.

I slept well for the first time in a long while that night and, when I woke, that wonderful feeling of calm you get wasn't immediately interrupted by thoughts of Al. That day, when I opened my eyes, the peace was followed by the knowledge that he was locked up. I would be OK.

That morning, Mum and David were anxious to get back to the house to see what the damage was; Mum was wondering what the term 'superficial' meant and whether the damage would be worse than she was expecting. Also we were all in dirty clothes and, in spite of showers, we were desperate to get back to our homes and get changed. However, the wait wasn't yet over. Court proceedings were scheduled for that morning so we spent another few anxious hours waiting to hear if Al would remain in custody. Al was in court in Brighton that morning and we were to be detained for our safety until he was remanded.

Finally the news came that he had been remanded in custody pending psychiatric assessment on the Monday, two days from then.

We went back to my flat and then set out for Aston Abbotts. I needed to see the house and see what Al had done to believe the fire had actually happened. At that point it was still almost as if it wasn't real. We had instructions to go to the local police station in Wing so we could be escorted back to my mum's house by the duty officer. The house was still taped up, so they thought it would be a good idea for us to be accompanied.

When we finally got back to the house we discovered an enormous roll of charred ivy in the front garden revealing scorched brickwork right up to the thatch. At the side the door was boarded up and inside we saw that only the frame remained of the half-glazed wooden door. The main thing was the fire had not got to the thatch, although it must have been a damn close thing.

Seeing the house for the first time and my mum's eyes filling with tears was a particularly difficult moment for me. I felt so responsible for everything that had happened; as I saw it, that fire was a direct result of some of the choices I had made. I wish I had acted sooner, or sorted things out quicker, or hadn't let certain things happen. I felt so ashamed. This was our home, our safe haven, and now it would never be the same.

As we walked through the smoke-stained door, all the surfaces and the floor were covered with a thin film of dirty ash. Mum burst into tears. I knew she'd been trying to fight her emotions and when they finally got the better of her it was like a floodgate had opened. David came and hugged her and stroked her hair. I had to get out of the house then. I knew I needed to see the damage but now I had I just wanted to get away and be anywhere but there. I just couldn't bear it, so I took Linus and we went for a long walk towards Cublington, a nearby village, down the country roads and footpaths which ran adjacent to farmers' fields.

As I strolled, I tried to take everything in. I knew that I had to take some time out just to try and let the knowledge of what had happened sink into my head somehow. I had been so shocked at every point of the ordeal: when he had refused to leave; when he had sent all the emails about us getting married; when I had come home on Christmas Eve and he had destroyed my things; when David and Paul had had to evict him; when he had come to see me at the flat and forced his way into my car; when he had sent the poison pen letters accusing me of murder and theft; and, finally, when he had set fire to the house and then been to the hospital to find me. But every time, I had found the strength from somewhere within myself to pull myself back up and keep going.

Suddenly, I felt as if I could barely stand; I no longer had the energy. It felt so surreal, as if my life had somehow taken a strange journey and I had been left behind, running to keep up.

I sat down on the damp grass with Linus sniffing the ground, and pulled off my socks and trainers. I needed to feel the ground on the balls of my feet. I sat there for a long, long time trying to feel some sort of connection to the world I was living in.

I organized three weeks off work and spent a couple of nights at home with Mum and David, but continued to battle my feelings of guilt about the damage to the house. One day I tried painting the board that now covered the side door to make it look better. In the garage I had found some paints and, through tears, I wielded an old paintbrush across the wooden board. I spent a lot of time sitting barefoot in the garden, trying to reconcile what had happened. When Paul invited me to spend some time with him and Linus on his canal boat on the Grand Union Canal, near Milton Keynes, I was happy to get away from everyone and everything. Paul left me to my own devices and cooked us simple meals, and we went on long walks in the countryside together.

Work had got in touch and had switched my placement from obs and gynae back to the GP's surgery I had worked in before, so it would be that much easier for me to return to because I was familiar with the systems and my role. It meant I could stop worrying about my career progression.

I surrounded myself with my family, eventually leaving Paul's and returning to my mum's house, where I had many heart-to-hearts with Mum and went with her to exercise classes and swimming sessions at Mentmore Country Club. Dave jumped on a plane from Australia and came to stay for a couple of weeks and I was happy to see his smiley, familiar face around the place.

After a few days I felt the need to go home to my flat in Brighton, to try and make sense of what had happened. But I remained strangely detached from reality, only answering the door when it was on the chain and often waking at night with my heart hammering and my eyes wide open. Every night before I went to bed, I searched the room and under the bed. In the mornings when I took a shower, I would never close the shower curtain – I had to see the exit; so every morning I would mop up the water which had filled the room. Sometimes my mind started to wander to dark places where I imagined that I or another member of my family had been killed and I tried so, so hard to block these thoughts out.

I have always loved a good detective drama, and one evening I watched an episode of *Midsomer Murders* in which one of the characters was killed by being bludgeoned around the head. I was fine while I was watching it, and it was almost farcical in its plot. But afterwards as I lay in bed trying to sleep, I began shaking and sweating and the torment continued for hours. I knew then that I had to stop watching these sorts of television programmes and would have to stick to innocent romantic comedies or period dramas. Anything with violence, suffering or murder tipped me over the edge. I also found watching the daily news really disturbing, especially if people were killed or there were violent crimes. I just couldn't cope with it.

There were often rude reminders of Al when we least expected them. A couple of weeks after the arrest, Gulshan rang my mum on the landline. She had arrived in London and was demanding that Mum or I come and pick her up and take her to Al. She seemed unsure what Al had been arrested for, but Mum – who was just as disturbed and horrified as me – simply gave her the number for Brighton police station. The conversation was both bizarre and worrying. Mum and David passed on the number she had called from and her photo to the police.

Every twenty-eight days Al had to go before a judge to see if he should be remanded in custody, and on each of these days I felt nauseous with nerves about what could happen. On one occasion I was told he had applied for bail and used my Brighton address as his place of residence. I was both amused and outraged at this but had Mum and David laughing when I declared, 'I suppose he expects me to pay his bail and then for him to come and live in my flat with me.' It was actually an accurate description of how deluded and crazy Al had become.

I thought this would be the end of it all. This just shows how little I knew. While he was in custody in Lewes prison, he continued to send me a few love letters. I don't know how they got through the censoring procedure but Al was very resourceful and they did. He managed to send through five before they stopped him. As soon as I saw the red envelopes sitting innocently on the doorstep I knew they were from him because of his distinctive, spidery handwriting. He disguised them by using different names: one was addressed to 'The Duty GP', while the others were made out to 'Dr Hewitt' and 'the solicitor', to try and disguise the fact he was writing to me. I never read them because I was scared of what they might contain. On one occasion, I ripped one corner off one of the letters just for curiosity's sake and then promptly phoned Emily, who shared my sense of frustration that even now he was firmly behind lock and key it appeared he hadn't been stopped from invading my life. No such joy. She reassured me that she would pass the message on to the prison that they needed to tighten up their procedures, and thankfully that was the last of the letters. I never found out what was in those letters; I didn't want to know.

Shortly afterwards we received a phone call saying that Al's trial would be in December 2011, which was followed up by an official-looking letter. I tried to blank it out and told myself I wouldn't think about it until nearer the time. But, of course, what had happened continued to haunt my every waking hour.

When I returned to Brighton at the beginning of May, I tried to get back to normal as far as possible. I think I had lost a sense of what 'normal' really was but I never wanted to take on the role of the victim and wallow in self-pity. I wrangled with continuous states of shock, disbelief, denial and sheer determination to carry on with my training. Mum, David and I continued to make our statements, adding extra details as we remembered them, and I met Emily a couple of times but my life felt vaguely settled for the first time in ages.

My supervisor at work, who was the head of GP training, was aware of what had gone on to some extent, so was kind and asked me regularly how I was feeling and if I needed any help or guidance. Work gave me purpose and the energy to hold back the tears and keep going, and to get up and on with my day like every other normal adult.

After about a month or so working at the GP's surgery, I was told that I had passed my academic year. It was based on coursework and assessments and the number of hours worked. I had had a fair amount of time out but I had managed to work the hours in elsewhere, and thankfully it had all been worth it.

There was still some uncertainty about what I would do next; I wondered whether I needed to take a year out to recover, rather than throw myself headlong back into hospital work. It was then, with no other immediate goal in sight and a few weeks with no plans until my next placement started, that I collapsed with raw exhaustion.

I had no energy to even think. A walk to the shops just a few minutes away would leave me shattered. I started to show signs of post-traumatic stress disorder, something which I never expected would happen to me. I would have flashbacks of hiding under the table in my flat, terrified and alone; I began imagining faceless motorcyclists in helmets whizzing past me ready to shoot; at night I became convinced there was someone in my flat wielding a gun, ready to pull the trigger as soon as they caught sight of me. Sometimes when

I was cooking I would pick up a knife to cut up some vegetables or a slice of cheese and suddenly have the realization
that there might be someone there, waiting to plunge it
into my chest. Was the knife meant for me? For a while I
had nightmares with similar thoughts, and I would wake
up sweating and scared. I learnt the movement of every
shadow in the flat and how it changed over the course of
twenty-four hours, and I was always ready to run should
something unexpected appear on the walls. I know Mum also
suffered with nightmares after the ordeal and I feel deeply
sorry for that.

I continued to see a counsellor and I found it helpful to
talk through everything. Slowly the images started to recede
and become less intense. The lady I saw taught me not to
'indulge' the thoughts and to accept them and move on, and
I was learning that if I didn't give them time, then they would
slowly start to be less frequent and intense.

I went on holiday to Malta with my mum in July and
despite everything that was happening in our lives we
managed to share some good times together. Slowly but
surely I began to heal. It was almost too hot with temperatures
of over 30 degrees and we were both knocked out by it, so
spent the whole time sleeping or relaxing underneath a
sunshade, reading books. It was a fairly average hotel with a
pool, and most days we just lazed around and went
swimming. We took a boat trip to a little island off Malta
called Gozo one afternoon, but in the main we were forced
to kick back and unwind, which was what we both needed. I
felt it was important for us to spend some time together

considering what we had been through, and it allowed us to reconnect away from home.

It was then that it really hit home how lucky I am to have such a supportive and loving family, and this proved to be a real turning point for me. After returning to the UK, the signs of post-traumatic stress I had been experiencing disappeared and, while I was still anxious, tired and in shock, the terrifying visions no longer haunted me.

In August I went back to the hospital to do my obs and gynae placement – where I should have been when Al came into the hospital. It was a tough placement, because while the midwives supervised the straightforward births we were always there when things were complicated, like when women needed caesareans, or when the women or babies were in trouble. Often it was quite hard, especially when women went into labour very early or there were problems with the babies. Starting out, it was very emotionally charged and we often saw incredibly raw grief, which was awful.

As well as births, I also ran early pregnancy clinics, where we saw miscarriages, ectopic pregnancies and women with heavy bleeding. It was difficult but the midwives were good fun, I enjoyed the company of the other doctors and there didn't seem to be the power struggles that I had envisaged. I was gradually slotting into some sort of normal life again.

Some days passed when I didn't think about my ordeal all the time, but Al was still like a constant shadow in my life. One day when I was working on the maternity ward, one of the security guards rang up to tell me that Al was downstairs in A&E in handcuffs. I was so shocked I actually had to sit down for a few seconds to let it sink in. With him away in prison, it felt like he was nowhere near me, yet here he was downstairs, just a few hundred metres away. I felt so relieved that I wasn't in the A&E department at the time and that his face was well-known within the security team. Initially I thought he might have been brought in because he was suicidal, which despite everything that had happened made me feel quite sad. In the end, I concluded that he had probably been beaten up by his fellow inmates, but I didn't find out. I didn't want to know. I can imagine that he could very easily wind other people up and if he was aggressive to others in there, no doubt they would fight back – and then some. I completed the rest of that shift nervously praying that I wouldn't be called down to A&E for any reason and no pregnant women would head there in the last stages of labour – because I would have to explain why I couldn't do my job and I hoped I had put the fear behind me, at work at least. I was determined to get through this block of work without having any drama.

In my free time, I decided to do more exercise, because it would boost my spirits and help me lose weight. I found the stress of the ordeal meant I had put on weight and I no longer felt that happy with myself physically. I took up boxercise, an exercise class based on the concepts boxers use to keep fit, two or three times a week. Along with a load of other people, I found myself doing lots of kicking and punching into thin air, and sets of star jumps, and I always emerged sweating, with a face like beetroot, buzzing with endorphins and feeling good. I discovered that it was a great way to channel my stress and that it made it easier for me to cope with work. I didn't use any free time to see old friends. I had retreated into a somewhat lonely existence then, but at this point it was on purpose: I knew I needed to focus solely on myself to continue getting over what had happened. I was still figuring things out and working out how I wanted my life to move on.

At the end of November, I had made plans to take time off work for the trial. It actually came round very quickly, but I still felt quite numb and had been trying to block it out. We had been told it would last two weeks and would involve sixty-four witnesses and countless bits of evidence. It was just a few days before it was due to start when a court officer called and told me it had been delayed until January because they were concerned that, given the complex nature of the case, it wouldn't conclude before Christmas. She sounded as if she was almost in tears, having made all the arrangements with every witness involved and then having to call round to each one to break the news. Mum and David said they felt cheated as they had psyched themselves up for it. But I don't think I had properly faced the reality that it was going to happen, so all I felt was relief that I could just enjoy my Christmas and not have to think about it for another few weeks. Deep down, though, I knew it was only delaying the inevitable and in a few weeks' time he would be facing the court to relay his version of the story.

He had pleaded not guilty to the charges: four counts of harassment against Mum and me, two for aggravated harassment, putting us in fear of violence, and two alternative counts of harassment; two counts of arson, one to the family home and attempted arson on Wing police station; possession of an offensive weapon (the loaded crossbow found in his car in the car park of the hospital at Haywards Heath); two counts of theft (my belongings and the coat and stethoscope at the hospital); and finally he was up for perverting the course of justice because he wrote to me in prison and, even though I personally never found out what he'd written, clearly he had intended to derail the case.

I also knew that it wouldn't be long before I would have to take to the stand and tell my story. It was as if *I* was going on trial as I faced the man who had made our lives a living hell.

Twelve

The Court Case

The trial of R v Al Amin Dhalla began in Court 4 at Lewes Crown Court on Monday 16 January 2012.

Mum and I were the first witnesses, but before taking evidence the two barristers outlined their cases for the prosecution and the defence. We had to wait in the prosecution witness waiting room until we were called to the stand. After giving evidence we were advised by the police not to remain in the courtroom as this might give the wrong impression to the jury. However, we all needed to know how the case was going and what was being said. There was still a chance he might get off and we were keen to hear more about the police investigations, which had taken months. So, after giving his evidence, David decided to stay to see it through and report back the events of each day.

Paul wanted to come down for the case, too. In the end, Paul stayed with me at the flat and Mum and David stayed at a hotel opposite the court. I think, with Dave in Australia and Mark in Norway, Paul felt that he needed to bring some of the strength that Dad would have brought. I realize that through what happened with Al, our relationship has really flourished and he is still always there when I need him most.

I had ended my stint in obs and gynae earlier in December and started in orthopaedics back at Haywards Heath Hospital. Thankfully, I managed to switch some shifts so my days off would coincide with the trial and got away with only booking a few days' leave. The placement in orthopaedics centred around people who required hip and knee replacements, but my job was mainly aftercare, so sorting out their medical needs while the physios got them back on their feet. It was relatively undemanding, which was a relief considering what was about to take place in my personal life.

Mum and I had asked for 'special measures' while we were giving evidence in court and this request was accepted. These measures are in place to help vulnerable witnesses give the best evidence they can and to relieve some of the stress associated with being in court. It meant that I would be able to see the jury and the judge, but there would be a screen up so I wouldn't see Al and he wouldn't be able to see me. I was hugely thankful for this. I couldn't imagine looking into Al's eyes after everything that had happened. Once the trial started it was clear that these measures were needed because Al began to give Paul what David called his 'predatory stare' and the judge had to ask Al to stop. Eventually they had to ask Paul to move to a place in the court where Al could not see him.

I was told I wouldn't be required to give evidence until the afternoon of the second day, which felt very strange because I felt that until then, everyone else was hearing about what had happened to me and the relationship, yet I couldn't be there to witness it, which was frustrating. Half of me wanted to be there, listening to what was being said, observing what the jury looked like and how the barristers were performing, yet the other half wanted to just shy away from the whole thing and pretend Alison Hewitt was someone else completely.

The prosecution barrister, Richard Barton, who I was first introduced to on the morning the case started, was just like something out of *Judge Judy*. His voice and projection would be right at home on the West End stage and, except for the fact he resembled a slightly younger version of the cartoon character Penfold, I could just imagine him starring in *Les Misérables*. He was jovial, chatty and very human and came over to us to explain exactly what would happen and how the events would unfold.

As a witness, I had to stay in the prosecution witness waiting room until I was called to give my evidence. We were not allowed to discuss the case with the other witnesses, needed an electronic combination to go to the loo and could only exit one at a time, to stop us conferring – there were legal officers around to make sure we didn't talk. Until Mum had given her evidence I knew I wasn't permitted to talk to her about it, which was really hard. I knew she had been through a terrible ordeal too and I wanted to support her.

*

Finally, after being expected to give evidence on the Tuesday and waiting nervously to be summoned, I was eventually called to the witness stand on the Wednesday morning at 10 a.m. The court usher led me through a series of corridors, like a rabbit warren, until we reached the judges' chambers and then the courtroom itself. The jury sat in front of me; a sea of faces of different ages, colours and nationalities. Looking back, it feels like such a blur but I remember the constant churning in my stomach and the fact I had to keep my arms and hands by my sides because they were shaking so much. My throat felt dry and I felt an intense pressure in my head. It was not lost on me that these people would decide Al's fate and therefore my own. If Al got off, I had no idea what the future might hold. I tried to read the subtleties in their faces, and to imagine the jobs they did or how sympathetic they might be; I wondered if they had families and daughters, but I came up blank. I knew I could only do my best – answer the questions and give the truest version of events possible.

I spent two-and-a-half days on the witness stand and everyone was surprised by how long I was up there. By the time I had arrived, the jury had been given a huge amount of detail and evidence. Everything had been collated in a big book and we were instructed to turn to various pages and look at the different exhibits, like maps and photographs, while the prosecution or defence made different points. I had to detail the whole relationship from the beginning and much of what was said was very personal. Al's barrister, who I found waffley and incoherent, read a selection of the love letters Al had sent me out to the courtroom and by the third letter, it just felt pointless as he relayed how much Al loved me or what we had done on a date while we were still together. The defence also recited some silly rhymes we had made up about each other. I felt so mortified and my skin crawled with humiliation.

The hardest questions were the ones where I was asked about why I hadn't dumped him sooner, why I had gone to Canada, why I had continued to speak to him, where the defence barrister had accused me of 'leading him on'. It almost felt like I was defending myself and as though I was on trial, not Al. I tried to give honest answers about how I had felt at the time and how the relationship had played out, but it was so, so hard. My body remained rigid throughout and my shoulders felt rock hard with tension. I didn't notice it at the time because I was so fired up with adrenaline, but afterwards I had such a splitting headache I could barely function. I felt so many different emotions at once – terror, fear, humiliation, anxiety, shame, panic and horror.

Al's barrister made very long-winded comments. He gave no detail and skirted around every point, going off on wild tangents that weren't at all related to the case. We thought for a while that his tactic might actually be to confuse everyone so much that the jury wouldn't know what point was being made. It was clear that everyone, including the judge, was being driven mad by him. Apparently the judge wasn't allowed to be too firm in hurrying anyone up, in case he could be accused of bias.

One of the worst moments for me was when I flicked

through the various pieces of evidence and my eye rested on the pictures of the weapons that had been in Al's van. I remember feeling complete disbelief, before the brutal reality hit me. That was what got me most of all: what he had planned to do with those weapons, how he had planned to get revenge. I started crying and the judge ordered a break in proceedings. I know Mum found it really hard that she couldn't comfort me because she was up next so we couldn't talk.

My questioning finally wrapped up on the Friday and I was pleased that at least my part was over. My neck and shoulders were so tight with stress afterwards I couldn't even get my arms into my coat.

The following Monday, Mum took to the stand. The defence attacked her, but I later heard she gave as good as she got. The classic moment during her questioning occurred when the defence asked her what qualifications she had to describe Al as a 'narcissistic psychopath'. Mum backtracked, saying it was always dangerous to label people.

The judge intervened, 'Let us hear what qualifications Mrs Hewitt does have.'

Mum answered, 'Well, I have a degree in psychology; I also trained as a social worker and a probation officer and worked in prisons and psychiatric hospitals.'

The defence quickly changed the subject.

After a day or so, the court went through the same motions with David in the witness box. Much was made by the defence barrister about how Al had been 'evicted' from my flat. Al's version of events was that Paul held him down, while

David beat him up and then they stole his wallet. He also accused David of making a racist remark as he left. The accusations were quite laughable.

I wasn't there to witness the rest of the case – only David remained in the public gallery – but there were still many witnesses who went on to speak to the court, including the letting agent who rented out Al's flat over the road from mine, the private investigator Al hired to spy on me, the farm worker who had originally spotted Al firing the crossbow in the Wiltshire field. The man who sold Al the van also took to the stand and confirmed that he had asked for modifications to be made to it, including removing the rear window and part of the front grill, so he could get from the front into the back seats. He had apparently told him that he wanted to use it as a camper van and that he suffered from claustrophobia, so he needed more air. When he was asked why he didn't just open the front windows, Al had made a further excuse.

Everyone who saw Al in Mum's village was questioned, along with various police officers and the doctors who had seen Al in the hospital on the day he was eventually caught by the police. There was even a woman from the Half Moon dating agency, who had conducted Al's interview to join this new agency after we had split up. He was, she said, 'a man in a hurry' and he didn't want to listen to what she had to say.

Then Al had his turn and was on the stand for almost five days. It was hard to hear David and Paul recount what had happened and not to have been there to witness what was being said myself. I knew Al was charming and intelligent, and my biggest fear was that he would come across as credible and persuasive. I felt strangely compelled to ask them everything he had said to the court word for word. I'm aware they tried to keep much of it from me but I wanted to know the truth. Among many other things, he told the jury we were like Romeo and Juliet. He told so many lies, stating among other things that Mum had ruined our Christmas together and threatened to call the police if I didn't return to Aston Abbotts, and that she was trying to organize an arranged marriage between me and Nick. He also continued to claim I had been stealing drugs from the NHS for several years; that Paul was into drugs and on one occasion, when he had stayed with me in Brighton, we went to a rave party (with drugs); and that Mum had been harassing both me and Gulshan in Canada. He also maintained that I had murdered the man in the hospice.

Parts of the trial went like this extract, recorded by David:

Prosecutor: *Alison said she was emotional when she found her certificate torn up in the bin.*

Al: *She was lying.*

Prosecutor: *If someone took things that were dear to her, including her butterfly picture, things that meant a lot to her – they were above the bed, special – she would have been upset if they were broken. She was proud of her degree certificate. How would you feel if your MBA certificate had been destroyed?*

Al: *I would have got another.*

Prosecutor: *You did it, did you not?*

Al: *No.*

Prosecutor: *She found a large number of documents missing after 8 January.*

Al: *I strongly suspect that Pam was the culprit.*

. . .

Prosecutor: *The drugs you found, tell us about them.*

Al: *Alison had been stealing drugs from the NHS for several years.*

Prosecutor: *Were they for her?*

Al: *She was giving them to her brother Paul.*

Prosecutor: *This woman has killed; appears to be a drug dealer. Why did you stay with her?*

Al: *Her mother coached her to tell lies.*

Throughout his questioning, Al seemed to have an answer for everything. He had found the stethoscope and doctor's coat on the floor when he went into the hospital for the first time and planned to return them on his second visit, and that could not be classified as theft. He claimed all the bizarre tools in the cars were 'vehicle-related'. Every single piece of information was pulled apart, analysed and put back together. When I heard what Al had said, and how he had a feasible-sounding argument for every question put to him, I wasn't sure if he would be found guilty. My main concern was that he might not be found guilty of arson – the most significant crime, which would carry the longest stretch of time in prison. It was the severity of this crime that meant the case was being heard at the Crown Court rather than at a magistrates' court.

After Al stood down, the trial was on the home straight and both the defence and the prosecution laid out their cases to the jury. I was told that the prosecutor spoke for just less than an hour, without a script. David said he was word perfect. One of the most chilling things he said was:

He conducts recces around Bedfordshire, Buckinghamshire and Sussex. He bought a rifle, a handgun and ammunition plus two crossbows and a number of crossbow bolts. He buys a van to which he makes strange modifications. Make of this what you will. He is planning a visit to the West Country and although we find no reference to Lundy he is planning to stay on the mainland during Pam and David's holiday on the island. If he has not planned to go to Lundy was he planning to be waiting for his nemesis Pam when she got off the boat? This is a case filled with coincidences.

And he concluded with the words:

Back at Haywards Heath, leaving the crossbow and knife in the car, he sought Alison. Was he going to abduct and harm her? He had identified a remote location nearby. Consider what he intended to do but for the intervention of the armed officers.

The defence made his speech – a more long-winded affair – and the jury filed out.

While the case was going on the press interest had seriously ramped up. One of the first journalists to get to know us was Mark Sanders, a BBC reporter on the south coast. He attended the trial on a number of occasions and when we talked to him he encouraged us to speak to the press, saying that we could either tell the truth or that it would be made up anyway. At first Mum and I were reluctant to be cast as 'weeping victims' but after talking about it we decided to take part in a post-trial press conference at Lewes police station, to highlight the issues of stalking. I gave a short statement and then Mum and David spoke, putting particular emphasis on thanking the police, the rapid reaction of the fire service and the fast response of the neighbours.

The first time I saw the story in the press it was so surreal; it was almost as if it wasn't me they were talking about. I don't know why but I got the impression they wouldn't use my name, but of course there were loads of pictures of Al and me together, on dates, holidays and in the flat. The *Independent* also published a picture of me in my swimsuit during my time with Al. I was horrified but fortunately I was wearing a big hat and glasses and the snap was in black and white, so I doubt people would have been able to recognize me.

Most of my friends knew that I was involved in a court case but I hadn't talked much about the detail of it. I had told different people various parts of the story but I was so worried that I wasn't supposed to talk about it that I had kept quiet on the whole. No one knew about the weapons Al had been in possession of, or the fact he had previously been in prison, but many knew that he had set fire to the house and had come to find me in hospital, dressed as a doctor. I hadn't wanted anything to stand against me when it came to the court case; as far as I was concerned, my friends would probably find out the truth later on. When they did eventually find out the true extent of Al's actions, most of them could not believe what I had been through. Their reactions ranged from not knowing what to say, to wanting to ask me lots of questions about my ordeal. They were all very sympathetic and rallied round, and I am truly grateful for their support.

Later a production company called Popkorn got in touch and the story became the subject of a one-hour documentary, *Living With My Stalker*, which aired on Channel 4 later in the year. The team behind it were great; they weren't intrusive, but I felt like they had got to the heart of the story and the terrifying ordeal that we had all endured.

The jury took twelve hours and forty-four minutes to reach their decision and the judge commended them on their high level of concentration, dedication and enthusiasm. Apparently a number of hardened court watchers said they were unusual in their attention and the number of pertinent questions they raised during the trial.

I sat in the waiting room, desperate to hear the verdict. Due to the special measures I was unable to be present in the courtroom. I held my breath and dug my fingernails hard into my palms, almost drawing blood, as the jury relayed their decision.

They had found Al guilty of seven counts, including arson and harassment of Mum and me. I felt almost numb but a dull wave of relief washed over me. They had found him not guilty of the theft of my property. Al had blamed my mum for the thefts and, without any of the items having been recovered, there was no evidence.

After these conclusions were read out, I exhaled quickly and forcefully. As the news started to slowly sink in, the numbness began to lift and I felt delighted, overwhelmed and overcome, and tears pricked my eyes. I knew it wasn't over but we were a good way there.

The sentencing would take about six weeks. The judge said he would call for a psychiatric report, which is mandatory in the case of arson, and a report from the probation service. He also said he would consider Mum's and my victim statements, extending the restraining order against Al, seizure of his assets and destruction of the weapons. It was later suggested to Al that if he gave permission to edit his website and remove pictures of me, it might be looked on favourably by the judge. But he never did.

I know Mum and David were very angry and frustrated that, given his violent criminal background, Al had been given a UK visa and been allowed to enter the country. If the UK Border Agency had made the necessary checks then our paths would never have crossed. Worse still was the fact that five months before Al went on the rampage, they had complained to the Home Secretary, Theresa May, passing on all the information provided by the private investigator about his violent past and prison sentences in Canada. They expressed grave concern that he was posing a threat to the safety of the family. They also informed her that Al had been refused entry to the USA and had a ten-year Weapons Prohibition Order placed on him as a result of his crimes in Canada. Sadly no one saw fit to contact them and no action was taken to detain him and deport him. They subsequently submitted a formal complaint to the Parliamentary and Health Services Ombudsman. They were terrified that once he was released he would be allowed to stay in the UK.

Mum and David were right to still be terrified of what Al could do. One day when I was at work, I had a call from Emily. She needed to talk to me urgently, so was coming in to see me. Again, my heart flipped. What could be so urgent? Was Al being let out? Had he been granted bail?

When I saw her, I could tell she was concerned and was not her normal, cheery self. A more senior officer accompanied her and there was a distinct look of pity in her face. The police had made a discovery, she said, and they thought I could be at risk. It was potentially very serious. They couldn't tell me what was going on; just that I was only able to go home briefly to get some belongings and the police would escort me to a B&B.

'I'll tell you more when I can,' Emily said, and I could tell that despite the close bond we had formed she was doing her job and had to take a step back.

Well practised at moving out quickly by this point, when I got back to the flat, I took all my important documents as well as my laptop and some DVDs. I knew I would need something to do. I didn't understand how this could be happening again. We had only just been in court and Al was behind bars.

Emily told me that Mum and David were being told the same and advised that they should stay somewhere else that night just in case. I moved into a nearby B&B and slept fretfully, waking every half hour or so, imagining I could hear someone in the bathroom or outside the door. Sometimes in the corner of my eye, I would catch a flash of something and spin round, only to be met with nothing. I had no idea what was happening and why the police thought I could be at risk, but I knew it must be serious.

The following day, Emily called me again and she told me that I should spend another night there. She confirmed that the risk was real: they believed someone had been hired to cause harm to 'one of the ladies involved in the case'. The prison staff had recorded a phone conversation between Al and his mother in Canada and, when they translated it, they realized Al was asking Gulshan to send a large sum of money to the UK. Al later claimed that it was an old debt he wanted to settle but the police looked into it. Two men – one who was on remand from Lewes prison where Al was being held – and a woman were arrested. The police suspected the money was intended to pay for one or all of these people to hurt Mum or me. In the end, the police decided that there was insufficient evidence to charge Al with conspiracy to murder.

It was devastating. I started shaking and crying. *'One of the ladies' – what did that mean? Me? My mum? Emily?* We'll never know.

This piece of news changed everything. I realized then that I would always have to watch my back. I could never totally trust anyone again. I would never, ever get away from him. Did he want me dead, or my mum dead? We would never feel safe.

I had finally hit the bottom of what was the worst experience I could ever imagine.

I couldn't live like that, working then having to tell one of my managers that I was leaving halfway through a shift, so I spoke to my managers and was given some leave. Mum and I decided to go and stay in the flat Dave owns in Putney, which Al had never visited. Dave was renting it out while he was in Australia but at that time it was empty and it seemed like a good solution. Mum and I holed up there and sobbed together, trying in vain to watch TV to distract ourselves from the reality of what was happening. Paul had become a tower of strength and as well as sorting out various things at my flat, like the broken boiler, he also came up to spend some time with us to try and make us feel more secure by having a man – and a large dog – in the place.

However, every face that I saw, old or young, black or white, could now be someone who wanted to do me harm. I didn't answer the phone when it rang unless it was family calling. I left people knocking at the door and I scurried from place to place with my head down and my shoulders hunched. I didn't want to be a victim but that was exactly what I was.

Eventually, Mum bought me a ticket to go out to see Dave in Australia. The police advised us that this would be a good course of action until they could establish the risk towards me.

Dave met me at Sydney airport and hugged me very hard as I sobbed into his shoulder, exhausted. I spent a couple of weeks trying to distract myself from everything that was happening at home by going to see the typical tourist sites, enjoying the warm weather, swimming in the apartment's pool and sleeping as much as I could. There was no new information from the police while I was there, and this was frustrating; I felt depressed and like I was in some kind of limbo, hanging by a thread from the precipice of some huge catastrophe.

Just before I went away, Mum, David, Paul and I had a meeting with the witness protection team, two men called John and Stuart. I had watched TV crime shows in the past, where the term was bandied around and courageous witnesses would be ferried off to a new life, away from dirty underworlds or criminal gangs.

The premise of what they suggested was simple: Mum, David and I would all change our names and move house, somewhere that we had no connections. I would pack a bag, get in the car and drive away. I would never return to my flat in Brighton or to my childhood home in Aston Abbotts. Essentially the past would cease to exist; Alison Hewitt would be no more. Paul was thought to be safe due to his nomadic existence, and anyway the targets were clearly Mum and me. At that time, all I could think about was being safe, and free from fear, from looking over my shoulder every few seconds and from that awful, gut-wrenching knot that lay permanently in my stomach.

They explained that people going into witness protection are required to sign a memorandum of understanding with the police. This is a legally enforcing document which bestows 'protected person' status and sets out the police's duty in protecting the witness. However, it also binds the witnesses to certain compromises in terms of lifestyle and access to family and friends. So I wouldn't be able to go and visit Dave in Australia and I would be limited in what I could do. There would be restricted access to Mark in Norway and my nephews. I wanted to see the boys grow up and to spend time with my brothers. I would be able to visit friends from time to time but they wouldn't be able to come and see me in my new life – it would be too risky. The life I would live would probably be a far more modest one, but then how important are material possessions?

I would potentially have to move countries and, after all my hard work, switch careers, but as I considered everything that was at stake, this was a sacrifice I felt I was willing to make.

For a long time, the idea was an appealing one. Regardless of the number of times I turned the question over in my head, I always came back to the same conclusion: I had had enough of being petrified, of waiting to see someone in uniform walk into the hospital, of hearing my mum scared. How could I continue living any sort of ordinary life without opting for witness protection? I couldn't.

I know Mum and David were considering their options too. They presumably felt a lot of the fear that was consuming me and as well as having a police car sitting outside their house for a number of days, they had four CCTV cameras installed around the exterior of the house. They were leaving nothing to chance. They were thinking around the subject of their new lives too: what would happen to Gulshan? Should she not be investigated for providing Al with the money? If the prison authorities cut off Al's funding from her then surely their risk would be less? Why should we remove ourselves from the risk, rather than have the risk removed from us? I know that even now they are putting off making a decision until nearer the time Al is released, and witness protection is definitely still a viable option to them and one that they are not ruling out.

As far as I was concerned at that time, I was just trying to pull my life back together in any way I could, as was Mum. While she fretted and sought reassurance from the police and her contact there, Lynda, I found myself lacking any sort of energy when it came to thinking about the future and dealing with what might happen. In the end, David took control and said he would be the central point of contact for all police-related matters.

On my return from Australia, I told Mum and David that I had made up my mind to go into the witness protection scheme, change my name and cut myself off from the life that I had known. If the threats were going to keep happening, if every time I thought I was finally free I would once again be reminded that I would never be free of Al, then I had had enough.

I didn't attend the court on the day of Al's sentencing on 29 June because I didn't want to antagonize him. Mum, David and Paul all went to the court to see the result. However, I later heard that the judge said the psychiatrist's report stated that Al did pose a significant risk to both Mum and me and the risk of violence in potential future relationships was high.

Al did not want any treatment, nor did he respond to it when it was given, and any future violence could be grave and severe. They concluded that he had what I had suspected after my stint in psychiatry: a 'narcissistic personality disorder'.

The judge explained that no further action could be taken regarding the alleged 'conspiracy to murder' plot and Al's suspected attempt to hire a hitman because there wasn't enough evidence. It was only touched upon briefly and we all felt frustrated that nothing else could be done about it.

Medical notes suggested that he was a suicide risk and that he had made attempts to hang himself from the door with his bed sheets and then a TV cable, which explained why he had been brought into A&E when I was at work that time.

However, he had also converted to Christianity while on remand inside Lewes prison, and had been both baptized and confirmed into the church. We knew this had happened during the trial because he wore a large crucifix around his neck but he took it one stage further and even had good character notes from three clergymen.

After even more notes and deliberations, the judge concluded that for the most serious crime of arson he was given eight years. For the attempted arson a further four years giving twelve years in all. He was sentenced to five months for each count of harassment, eight months for damage to property, three years for possession of an offensive weapon, six months for each count of theft of the white coat and stethoscope, and two years for perverting the course of justice. He was told he must serve a minimum term of six years, less the fifteen months he had already spent in custody. The parole board would have to be satisfied that he was no longer a threat when he was released.

When Mum called to tell me how long Al's sentence was, I felt quite tearful with relief that it was over. I had felt incredibly anxious all day, glancing at my phone every five minutes, willing it to ring so I could be put out of my misery. When it finally did ring and Mum told me, I just felt the tears running down my cheeks as she spoke. At least I didn't have to do anything immediately. I had time to consider what I wanted in the future and whether I would change my name or move out from my flat. I felt safer, knowing he was inside and even now I am kept in the loop about his various appeals and things that rumble on in the background. Some days I manage to not think about it at all, so these pieces of news serve as an ugly and stressful reminder of what happened.

Whichever way I look at it, I know Al will serve his time for what he has done to me and leave prison able to begin his life over again. However, for me, this will be my life sentence.

Epilogue

Looking back on this experience, I know I will never be free from fear. There will always be a risk, as we believe Al will continue to hold a grudge against me and my family for the rest of his life. I will forever be looking over my shoulder and wondering if I am safe. Some days are worse than others: when innocent strangers come and ask me questions and I shy away from them, or when I see someone at work who has the same distinctive dark eyes and I am transported right back to that time when I feared for my life and the lives of the people I love the most.

Even now I struggle to believe everything that has happened. After the event, when I told people my story, they often looked at me in disbelief, as if I was making it up for attention, and said that it seemed too far-fetched. I know all too well that it happened but I have to remind myself to stop myself from blurting everything out.

I think I shut down emotionally for a long time during the

whole ordeal, and it is only more recently that I have started to think about how I want my life to be going forwards. I do know I will never be the carefree person I once was, and I mourn the untroubled and vivacious part of myself, which I have lost forever. My counselling sessions have helped me deal with it. I have seen different people and while there have been gaps in time when I haven't regularly gone to sessions, I know now that it's a good thing and that it helps me tremendously.

For a while I didn't even think about dating again and resigned myself to the fact that, at thirty-seven, with a huge amount of baggage and trust issues, it would likely be an uphill struggle to form any sort of lasting relationship. However, I gave myself a good talking to about it. I decided I could turn into a bitter, man-hating person whose life and relationships with men would be defined by my experience with Al, or I could move on and hurl myself kicking and screaming past it in some way and make myself open to dating again. To give myself a fighting chance of having all the things I wanted in my life when I met Al. Ultimately I knew that I could never really move on until I met someone else and had another relationship. If I wanted revenge for everything Al did to me, then this would be the best form of payback in my mind.

A month after Al was sentenced, I went to a day-long relaxation and meditation course in a yoga studio behind Victoria Station in London. I figured that anything that could help me would be a good thing. It was a real mixed group of people of all ages and I was quite happy being anonymous and away from Brighton, where no one knew me or what had happened. Thankfully, we didn't have to talk about ourselves and why we were there, but we were divided up into groups and set different exercises designed to get our minds to focus and harness our emotions. I remember one activity was to just focus on a raspberry and look at it closely, describing the intricate structure, then smell it and talk about the different scents, then finally we could eat it but we had to properly taste it.

In another part of the course, we were paired up and told to write down the complimentary things about the other person on an envelope, be it the way their eyes crinkled in the corners when they smiled, or the fullness of their hair or their mouth. There were a couple of good-looking men on the course – including one who was also called Al. He was extremely tall at over 6 foot and stocky, like a bouncer, and at the time he had very short hair. I remember being surprised by his choice of footwear because he was wearing a pair of Crocs. (I later learned that he had recently had an operation on his ankle.) He was quiet and when I spoke to him there were a few silences but, out of everyone, I felt like we got on the best.

As the day drew to an end, the tutor gave us the opportunity to swap numbers with people we had spoken to or connected with during the day and I casually took Al's number and, a few days later, I texted asking if he wanted to meet up. I didn't really expect anything from it but his reply was overwhelmingly positive: 'Yes, definitely!' he wrote.

He was living in London at the time and obviously I was

still down in Brighton, and on the course we had talked about how we both liked going out in the countryside, so we agreed to meet in Ashdown Forest, which was halfway between us. Looking back, I'm pretty surprised at the date choice given what I had been through with Al mark one. Maybe I knew that this Al could be trusted, so I would be fine being in the middle of nowhere with someone who was barely more than a stranger.

We talked more about our lives. I told him about my work and he explained a bit more about himself. He was forty at the time and as well as a stint in the RAF he had had a big career in the City doing international law. I think he had had the City life, with the big bonuses, nights out and smart suits, but after about ten years he'd got sick of it and quit. He decided to take a gap year and do more hobbies and things he wished he had done as a child. Maybe it was some sort of midlife crisis but mountaineering and kayaking featured highly on his list of regular activities. He also did some youth work, with the Air Training Corps and the Duke of Edinburgh's Award, taking kids out on sports courses and teaching them how to read compasses.

I had gone wrong before when it came to judging men and I hated to think someone would pull the wool over my eyes again. As we walked, we were getting on well but I knew I had to tell him about what I had been through. It seemed wrong not to confess and I felt like we had some sort of connection. We sat on a big tree trunk and I told him that I wanted to tell him my story and so it would then be up to him to decide whether he wanted to see me again.

He was shocked, I know, but part of me was surprised at how well he took it. I think, given his background and his time in the forces, he had a different mentality. He had been trained for war, where bombs would be exploding around him and where there was loss of life. A few dates down the line, he then decided to tell me about his secrets; about the stuff he didn't like talking about that he had been through and had seen. Then it was all out of the way and we could concentrate on simply getting to know each other better.

I found it very easy to trust the second Al. I rationalized that what had happened before to me was so extreme, so serious and rare, that the likelihood of me falling foul of someone like that again was very small. I had my eyes wide open this time, but I was also aware that most people are good. Mum, David and my brothers all like him a lot too.

We moved in together at the end of 2013. We share a love of being outdoors and one day we will have a rural life, away from the busy cities of London and Brighton, and will enjoy a simple life together.

As far as my training was concerned, all my hard work finally came to fruition. After the stint in orthopaedics, where I had taken a substantial amount of time out after the hitman threat, I spent time doing ENT, treating conditions related to the ears, nose and throat, and then did another stint in the GP's surgery. In late 2013, I passed my final exams and became a fully fledged GP. It has been a hard slog but I love it like I thought I would when I was training, seeing different people every day and ultimately making a difference to the local community.

As the trial started to fade into the past, my focus started to shift and I began to think about how I could make a difference to other stalking victims. I knew the outcome of my experience could have been far, far worse and I started to question whether I could help others. While the police had been great when the situation had become serious, stalking wasn't seen as a crime. Yet it could happen to anyone. I always believe things happen for a reason, although I have yet to work out why this happened to me, but I have tried to give people the benefit of my experience, so at least some positives can be derived from it. At the time Al was sentenced, a British Crime Survey suggested that at least 120,000 individuals were affected by stalking and harassment each year but only 2 per cent resulted in convictions. Many people see glimpses of stalker-like behaviour within unhealthy relationships.

I have now stood up and told my story many times. After the press conference following the court case, Emily suggested I say something that might be useful to other stalker victims. I did a radio interview and also being interviewed was a criminal behavioural analyst called Laura Richards, who later got in touch with me after getting my details from the radio station.

After a decade working on violent crime at Scotland Yard, Laura was involved in setting up the National Stalking Helpline in 2010 and coordinated the UK's first National Stalking Awareness Week in 2011. In November 2011, she also published *The Victim's Voice*, a briefing from the national charity Protection Against Stalking (PAS) for an independent parliamentary inquiry into stalking law reform. It showed a 'deep dissatisfaction' with criminal justice professionals and a lack of confidence in the judicial system around the subject of stalking. It was clear that stalking was not recognized by the criminal justice system and that as a result it often went unreported. There was a pattern to stalkers' behaviour but it was often missed by the police and judges, and risk assessment, risk management and a coordinated response was lacking.

Victims have too often paid with their lives, such as Clare Bernal who was murdered in 2005 in Harvey Nichols by Michael Pech, Rana Faruqui who was stalked and murdered by Stephen Griffiths in 2003, and Jane Clough who was stalked and murdered by Jonathan Vass in 2010. In February 2011, Clifford Mills stalked his ex-girlfriend Lorna Smith on Facebook before stabbing her to death at his flat in Brixton. There have sadly been many more.

In November 2012, stalking became a specific criminal offence in England and Wales. The government introduced two offences: stalking and stalking involving a fear of violence. It was hoped that this distinction would provide greater clarity around the offence for the police and others looking to improve the safety of victims and bring perpetrators to justice. It went through parliament very, very quickly.

When I met Laura she told me that they now needed to train the police, and so training days were organized, for which I went into London and spoke about my experience and how things quickly escalated. It wasn't too difficult and in some ways it was cathartic. After going through the court case, I have found it easier to talk about what I have been through in a calm, factual and steady way.

I was put in touch with another victim. Her story is very different to mine. Her relationship broke down after she discovered her partner was on the sex offenders register for raping a fourteen-year-old girl. During the stalking he was arrested on many occasions, released on bail and spent some time in custody. He left his car outside her parents' house for days to intimidate her, called her constantly, broke into her house and once sent her an image of a noose.

Laura Richards, along with Allison Mann and Harry Fletcher, is a co-director of Paladin, a charity that aims to support high-risk victims of stalking and provides training and post-legislative scrutiny. During the charity launch of Paladin at the House of Lords, which I attended with Mum, I stood up and spoke about my case again to a room of over 150 guests and parliamentarians.

Laura summed it up when she said, 'A lot of people use the term "stalking" as a joke. But it's very similar to animals that hunt. It's about poaching, prowling, following. It's intrusive behaviour that engenders fear in another person. In other words, it's humans hunting humans.'

I hope that, in time, as the months and years pass and it becomes more distant in my memory, I will move on and leave this part of my life behind. I won't be defined by it and I refuse to let him turn me into a shy and nervous person who lives in the shadows. Now I have a job I relish, a man I love and a wonderfully supportive and strong family, who have weathered this horrific storm by my side and still come out smiling.

My world is a good one again.

Afterword

The year is now 2018. Time has moved on and a lot has happened since I first wrote *Stalked*. I have a strong relationship with a man I love dearly. I now live in a house in the country that we are decorating and I am deciding where to plant some apple trees in the garden. Country life has done us good; fresh air, walks by the sea and a new start has been just what we needed. My life now is calmer and so far removed from the events described in this book.

I'm not often asked about my experience of being stalked, but it does crop up from time to time. When I think back to what happened to me I still react with a large degree of shock. It was a crazy, crazy time and I'm still sometimes in disbelief that it ever occurred. I'm deeply saddened by the effects it had on me and by how, within a year of meeting someone, I had gone from a generally happy-go-lucky career woman to a shrivelling insecure wreck, in fear of her life and the lives of everyone around her.

There remains a degree of shame. I am still ashamed of the events that happened, both to myself and my loved ones. I regret that I didn't pick up on the signs of stalking earlier, that I didn't seek help from the amazing stalking support organizations in the UK that exist to help victims, and that I didn't run, move away or react differently to prevent these things from happening. However, hindsight is a wonderful thing and deep down I know that I just didn't recognize the signs of stalking until I was in too deep and that there is no running or hiding in stalking because, wherever you go, the stalker will find you, or ruin your relationships with your family, friends or workplace until they hunt you down. My actions were those of someone completely naive, someone suspecting that it was just a difficult relationship break-up, that she could deal with it all herself without asking for help, and that others wouldn't be affected. How wrong I was.

The following years after the court case I spent a lot of time working with the media. I did TV chat shows, documentaries, radio, magazine and newspaper interviews, as well as writing this book. The media loved the story. It was crazy, mad, sensational and filled with drama and emotion. I also did a lot of public speaking, describing what had happened to me and educating people on the signs of stalking and how to get help. My story as I told it then was raw and emotional, revealed by a woman whose confidence and life was in tatters and who was struggling to come to terms with why this had happened to her and how to move on, but it was also one of survival, of lessons learned. As I spoke to other victims and specialists educating about stalking, I began to realize that my story was important because it contained many of the tell-tale signs of stalking and how quickly things can escalate. I also began to realize how lucky I was to be alive to tell it. This work was incredibly powerful for me. My thoughts and actions were questioned and discussed. I received a lot of criticism but also a lot of praise and thanks for speaking. It was incredibly therapeutic work and probably formed some of the best counselling I could ever have received. I told the story and analysed it over and over again until my emotions began to calm and healing started to occur.

And it was at this point that, as I began to heal, I became less interested in this work. I faced a choice: whether to continue educational work and take the past forward with me in my life, or whether to cut ties and focus on a new life in the future. I chose to leave it in the past. To move forward, to rebuild new, positive memories with family and friends, to reconnect with my dreams for the future and learn how to live life again.

Of course, that said, I can never completely leave this behind. Mr Dhalla continues to be behind bars and for the moment I am safe. I know that there are no guarantees that that will be the case in the future.

But for now, I am enjoying my life in the countryside. I've regained my mental and physical health and I'm a much stronger person. I have family and friends who I love deeply and I've rebuilt my career as a family doctor. I have new hobbies and adventures planned to look forward to. People these days are often surprised when they discover that I was stalked. They are surprised by my attitude to life, that I'm not more down, depressed or insecure. My response is that I survived, my family survived, so how could I not be grateful for each and every day?